UNZIP

THE ADOLESCENT CHICK

FACING ALL YOUR TEENAGE CONCERNS AND
FEARS HEAD ON AND OVERCOMING THEM
TRIUMPHANTLY

ANN CARNI

BALBOA.
PRESS

A DIVISION OF HAY HOUSE

Balboa Press books may be ordered through booksellers or by contacting:

Balboa Press
A Division of Hay House
1663 Liberty Drive
Bloomington, IN 47403
www.balboapress.com.au
1 (877) 407-4847

Print information available on the last page.

ISBN: 978-1-5043-0572-3 (sc)
ISBN: 978-1-5043-0573-0 (e)

Balboa Press rev. date: 12/12/2016

To my four beautiful granddaughters Alannah, Sienna, Taylah and Jana may you grow into loveliness and happy free-spirited young women who know the joy of giving your all and shining your light into the darkness of this world.

CONTENTS

ACKNOWLEDGEMENTS

To those special persons in my life who melted in the back ground when I needed space to write my book. Many words of encouragement were offered from my husband Pete and who turned out to be my best critic. Special thanks to my adult children, Christopher and Karleen, who have been an inspiration and amazement to me in pursuing their own dreams and goals. Special mention goes to my amazing mother, Cordelia, who in her ninetieth year till is seizing every opportunity she can in life. Her determination and dedication has shown me that anything is possible.

To pursue my dream of writing *Unzip the Adolescent Chick*, this wouldn't have been possible unless a certain event hadn't taken place. There is always a reason for any situation, but at the time, falling and fracturing three bones in my ankle wasn't on my wish list or agenda. Without this happening I would not have the freedom to lay almost four months in bed recuperating and writing.

Special acknowledgements and thanks go to my own cheer squad who offered encouragement and advice along the way.

To all who read *Unzip the Adolescent Chick,* thank you for allowing me to share my amazing journey and insights with you.

Blessings and gratitude
Ann

INTRODUCTION

M y book has been envisioned in my mind for some years and has now been created through written words into reality. I penned my thoughts and emotions onto a notepad in the beginning, believing that as I reflected back, it would all make sense.

Having acquired plenty of knowledge through my life's experiences, this information needed to be shared specifically with teenage girls. Many of my mistakes because of wrong decisions as an adolescent could have been avoided if I had trusted and listened to my instincts or inner voice.

For many years I was completely unaware that my life was out of balance with my true self. By unzipping all your teenage concerns with the help of my experience, my aim is to dispel fear, doubt, and anxiety so you can move forward into action. It's possible to build healthy relationships, sustain good health, and have success, joy, and wealth in every area of your life through these uncertain times. You will find peace within yourself as you reach for your goals and seek your real purpose. You will find hidden golden nuggets that you can implement in your life right now that will benefit you.

I have included a variety of subjects that will help clear confusion on the most important decisions you will ever have to make as an adolescent. These decisions will have the greatest impact on your present and future.

This book is written especially for the adolescent chick in mind. Every word is expressed with love and authenticity.

I welcome you on this beautiful journey and together we will begin to unzip the shining light that is hiding within you.

Blessings and gratitude

Ann

UNZIPPED

Underneath the zipper, no leering eyes should see
Zippers are for covering, the innocence of me
Hardly surprising, the shocked look on your face
Dangerously exposed, and disgraced
Out of bounds of young, soft skin
There's nowhere to hide, only within
Nipples pink and hardened, tempting with seductive delight
My emotions I cannot hide, or fight
Fondling, eager hands, caressing, and adoring
My innocence of youth, unzipped,
With limbs, sprawling
Exposed, open, and displayed
Please don't judge
Or condemn me to a life not worth living
For I am young, curious and full of yearning.

CHAPTER 1

* * * * * * * ● ● ● ● * * * *

YOU ARE ENOUGH

A warm welcome to those who have chosen this self-help book. I am grateful for you allowing me the privilege to assist you during your adolescent years. My hope is that by reading these chapters, you will become a confident young woman, ready to tackle life with gusto and determination.

Has anyone ever called you stupid or used other derogatory names, making you feel like you're a worthless nobody? It's hurtful, right?

Your first thoughts are embarrassment and anger. Then you want to retaliate by lashing out at the other person, or you may feel completely numb and can't even speak.

These are all emotions you feel, so how do you handle yourself in a situation that calls for decorum and mature behaviour? First, you acknowledge these feelings, and with all your strength and power, try to stay calm. The simplest approach is to say something like, "Would you mind repeating that?" or, and walk away if possible.

In chapter 13, I walk you through how to set boundaries for yourself to become confidently reassured in a situation like this.

When someone says something horrible to another person, it's really about the person speaking, so don't take it personally.

Shy teenage Girl
Photo @Jose Antonio Sanchez Reyes/Dreamtime.com

When I was kindergarten, I was told by the choir teacher to stop singing and for everyone else to sing. Then, in front of everyone, the teacher looked at me and said, "She's the one singing out of tune." I wasn't even aware I was singing out of tune; I didn't have that concept as a five-year-old. Can you imagine how absolutely heartbroken I was? I believed I couldn't sing.

Do you think I got over this incident?

No way. I held onto the belief that I couldn't sing if my life depended upon it for many years. Children and teenagers are very impressionable, and while I think most parents, church leaders, and schoolteachers do good jobs, they forget the important fact that they are responsible for many shattered lives through senseless, hurtful words.

Some children and teenagers have been physically and mentally abused and let down badly by those in authority.

These young ones have mistakenly been classified as disruptive and labelled by many as troublemakers.

Now that you are a teenager, you have it on your own authority to not let others beat you down with their hurtful words and actions. So pick yourself up and dust yourself off because you are more capable than you have been led to believe. Acknowledging you are good enough just the way you are is the first step in empowerment.

As you approach adolescence and start making your own decisions in life, decide to stop allowing other people's circumstances and comments to rule you. The scars that we carry from hurtful words and physical abuse can last for decades. So please don't let other people's opinions or words steal your joy and happiness. Don't let circumstances define who you are. You are capable of being someone special.

You have to believe you are enough.

I grew up in a home with two parents and my two older brothers, Peter and Glenn. We siblings enjoyed a wonderful childhood.

My dad was a petty officer in the Royal Australian Navy and later an office worker in charge of superannuation at AIAS Port Kembla steelworks. My mum loved being the homemaker and was skilled in sewing, knitting, and crocheting.

We greedily indulged in her home style cooking and yummy pastry treats. Looking back now, I don't think we had a lot of money, but we never went hungry or without. My parents later enjoyed many years taking care of welfare children in family group homes in Sydney and left me in charge of our family home when I was around eighteen years old. They must have thought I was mature and responsible. How wrong they were.

During my high school years, I played basketball and hockey and enjoyed practice sessions and team games. As a teenager, I loved all the creative arts, like painting, pottery, dancing, knitting, and sewing. Unfortunately, I was always comparing myself to others and believing I wasn't good enough. We can never have our time again, but I would say to my younger self, "Keep practicing, and be a better version of yourself than yesterday." As a parent, I have always instilled in my children to do the best they can with what they have, keep going, and they will become better.

Even if you come last but tried your hardest, you are enough just by participating.

Learning a new skill takes practice, patience, persistence, and determination. It is all part of the journey. If someone offers criticism, and you don't agree with what they say, let the words wash over your head and keep doing what you're doing. If, on the flip side of the coin, the criticism is constructive and you agree it is helpful, that brings you closer to your goals.

The teacher who said I was singing out of tune never said I couldn't sing. The saddest thing is what I assumed she said and believed in my mind all these years. And it's sometimes true for all of us. The words and our thoughts get twisted, and we imagine stories or scenarios that never happened. When we look at our peers, we perceive them to be confident, perfect role models with ideal lives. This is not true. Most people are hiding behind the smiles, putting up good fronts.

We think others are looking at us all the time when actually they aren't; they have their own insecurities. The secret is to not let our emotions control us. As long as we acknowledge that we aren't perfect and are true to our feelings, we have the power to hide them from the world also.

Just look at some famous people. When they first started out, some were perceived by some as failures or not good enough.

Thomas Edison, who invented the light bulb, was told he was "too stupid to learn anything and fired from his first two jobs. He said, "I haven't failed; I've just found ten thousand ways that didn't work."

Oprah Winfrey had an abusive childhood and numerous career setbacks. While auditioning for her first job as a television reporter, she was told she was unfit for television. Wow, take a look at her achievements now. Do you think she listened to her critics? No, she went after something she wanted more than anything else.

Soichiro Honda was turned down by Toyota Motor Corporation for an engineering job, leaving him jobless for some time. He started building scooters at his home, and neighbours encouraged him to start his own business. Of course, it's now a billion-dollar business.

Stephen King is one of the best- selling authors of all time. This nearly didn't happen, because his first book, the thriller *Carrie*, received thirty rejections, finally causing him to throw it in the bin. His wife retrieved it and encouraged him to resubmit it. The rest is history.

Of course, everyone is familiar with the author J. K. Rowling, who wrote the harry potter books. This single mum's manuscript was rejected about fifty times before she had her first book published. Now she is living a dream life. She said, "I am enough," and believed in herself.

Although the irony is she never mentioned she was a woman. She only wrote her Christian name as initials, so the publishers just assumed whoever wrote the book was a man: a clever tactic. But it's such a stigma that women still have to resort to this ploy. It's shameful for this generation.

There are countless others who never stopped believing that they could change the world by making a difference.

Did they listen to others or give up on their goals, dreams, and hopes? No.

Can you imagine if these famous people had given up on their dreams and believed what others said about them and thought, they said I'm not good enough? How cheated the world would have been if they didn't show up, for they have enriched our lives forever.

It wasn't that long ago that white and coloured persons couldn't by law, associate together and were segregated.

In December 1955, Rosa Parks, an American black woman, defied the law by refusing to give up her seat to a white man. Three other black riders sat in the same row, one next to Rosa Parks, the other two across the aisle.

When the bus driver demanded that all four passengers give up their seats to white folks, the three other riders reluctantly got up. All the black riders were now at the back, and all the whites at the front.

Rosa Parks sat between them, a brave, solitary figure, marking the painful boundary between races. "As I sat there, I tried not to think about what might happen. I knew that anything was possible. I could be manhandled or beaten. I could be arrested. The time had just come when I had been pushed as far as I could stand to be pushed, I suppose. I had decided that I would have to know, once and for all, what rights I had as a human being, and a citizen."

Sometimes it's worth standing up for your principles and what's right. It's having the guts to believe in yourself; "I am good enough." Just as Rosa Parks believed that she and all black Americans have civil rights, you also are not to believe you're second class. You are worthy of a life of greatness. Never believe that you are beneath others; you are equal.

And sometimes we make mistakes so we can best learn from them. Fear of failure can lead to a stifled life, one of mediocrity, and you end up as an underachiever.

That's not living. Don't die with a song or painting still in you. Embrace life, boost your energy levels, have no fear of failure, take a risk, learn to grow, and try harder.

If you fail at first, don't give up. Change your approach, change the attitude, have fun and just keep going.

Whatever you do in your personal, school or career life, if you follow the above rules, you'll be on your way to become an achiever of your dreams. I had a dream to write a book for many years and now I'm living that dream, I stopped listening to my disbelieving words that I wasn't good enough.

- I want to encourage you to try new things.
- Stretch yourself and have some fun, because you don't know what you are capable of achieving until you try.
- Never listen to the irritating monkey chatter that's inside your head. That's the voice that wants you to fail and give up before you're even started. "You're going to fail, so why bother starting, you moron".

- The negative people in your life could be a parent, best friend, relative, boyfriend, schoolteacher or neighbour. Don't waste your time listening to them, walk away. Yes, it's a little difficult to walk out of a school classroom or walk out of your family home physically, but mentally you can. Just keep repeating silently to yourself, "I am enough," several times and you'll start to believe it.
- Don't be defined by your circumstances or someone else's.
- Never listen or give up on something just because someone says you suck at it. With practice and perseverance, you could be the next best computer programmer, inventor, writer, musician, or actress.
- Make it a habit every morning and every evening for thirty days to say to yourself, "I am enough," out loud so it becomes a habit.
- And you are enough, believe in yourself and with the right attitude you can achieve the impossible, so instil this in your conscious mind.

If God cares about the birds and flowers and every hair on your head, He must think you're worth everything. It all begins with saying these words, "I am enough," and yes, you are. You are born for a purpose, and my hope is you will find that purpose for your life. In chapter two, you may just find what you need.

CHAPTER 2

· ※ ⊛ ✦ ✦ ✦ ◆ ● ● ● ● ◆ ✦ ✦ ⊛ ※ ·

YOUR INTENTIONS AND DREAMS

Impossible is just a big word thrown by small men who find it easier to live in the world they've been given than to explore the power they have to change it. Impossible is not a fact. It's an opinion. Impossible is not a declaration. It's a dare.

Impossible is potential. Impossible is temporary. Impossible is nothing.

Muhammad Ali

I f you are like most adolescents, you'll have a never-ending list of goals and dreams you want to achieve. Maybe you want to have a career, own a company, be married, have children or travel the world seeking adventure. But before you charge full steam ahead and map out your life, it's best to take the roads with the least speed humps and traffic lights. Many of you will need the maturity to make grown-up decisions, but it's a little scary and stressful in an unknown world. Some of you may not even like making decisions, but in fact, not making a decision is a decision.

And there are some who just follow others like little lambs and do whatever their friends do or say.

If you are in the process of making a decision, always ask yourself, "is this the best option for me?" before making your final choice.

Some major decisions take longer to decide, so it's best to write down on a piece of paper all the positives and negatives. Does your decision feel right, or do you feel like your stomach is tied up in knots? I encourage you to think very carefully about your future as you prepare to make some of the most important decisions in your teenage years because those decisions may have a bearing on your future. Of course, nothing needs to be set in concrete; you can change your mind, and you do have free will.

What your friends have decided is no concern, you are your own person and capable of deciding what's best for only you. Of course, it's always good and advisable to have an adult's perspective or opinion on big decisions that will affect your future. Believe it or not, adults do have a lot of knowledge and expertise that you may not have even considered.

Write down your goals and dreams with the idea of reviewing them weekly to see if you are on track.

Dreams can be challenging, because they will involve imagination, work, and sacrifice on your part. Intentions can be dreams, but if you have veered off course a little, with good guidance you can get back on track.

We can all have good intentions, but without the follow-up steps towards your dreams, it will amount to zero.

I want you to fully participate in giving this exercise your best shot, so write down all your goals and dreams on a large sheet of paper.

No matter how unbelievable and out of reach you think they are, it will be well worth the effort.

So let's make this interesting. Can you come up with one hundred goals or dreams?

Also, never say a goal in the negative, for example, saying, "I want a partner who does not smoke or drink." It's better instead to say, "I would like a partner who is strong, fit, and well-toned and loves to workout at the gym."

This is the difference. Because you will attract what you think and say, always place your dreams in a positive frame of mind.

I am sure you will come up with lots of ideas. Don't be afraid to write down all your dreams and goals with a time frame next to it.

For example, if you wrote down, "I want a new haircut and colour," this could be a time frame of next week, but if you wanted to own a unit in Sydney, this may take you another fifteen years.

Just write everything down. Don't worry about how you are going to get it; this will unfold and become reality.

Now you have finished your list. Next, I want you to place your goals into different lists so that they are all categorized like subfolders on a computer.

So grab another sheet of paper, and on the top of the page, starting from the left-hand side, write down "career" or "study goal." And then going across the page, write "personal goal", then "dream goal", then "money goal," then, "health goal" and lastly, "contribution goal."

Career Goals

Now from the list on the first piece of paper, find what you wrote down as a career goal and write this under your career list and also the time frame. Imagine for this exercise you wanted to become a lawyer and it will take you seven years of study at the university, but you're only in year eight in high school.

It will take you eleven years, more or less, to finish studying and get your degree as a lawyer.

You say, "Oh no, this will take too long. Is this something that I really want more than anything else in the world? Am I willing to sacrifice my time for the next eleven years to fulfil my dream career?"

Listen, nobody said it would be easy. A degree is not handed to you on a silver plate, or else everyone would be doing it. It takes tons of time, effort, and focus to pursue your dreams and goals.

If it's a matter of money: then you will need to have a conversation with your parents about the affordability. Maybe they have saved money for your education, or you have obtained a scholarship to help pay for your school fees.

The other option is for you to apply for government assistance and repay the course fees when you have finished studying and have paid work. Now your course may not be available at your local university, so you will need to move away from home to do your studies.

Find out if you are eligible then go to Government Centre Link and apply for a full or part payment of the "living away from home student allowance".

All the planning may all seem a little overwhelming at first, but every dream is reachable. Perhaps deferring university for a year and working might be another option for you until you can cope better financially.

If plan A doesn't work, go to plan B
Photo @ Martinmark / Dreamtime.com

It is harder to start studying again after a few years' break, but not impossible if you have set your mind on your dream. I've done it, and I'm still studying, so never say you're too old for learning anything.

If it's over ten years since you finished school, you will need to do the entry course before you are accepted into university. Otherwise, technical colleges or online study offer good pathways to obtain higher education. Any courses you do will be credited to you with your own unique USI number till you reach your goal.

If this is your goal that you desperately want to achieve your dream, then you will find a solution.

When I was sixteen, I wanted to be a beautician, as I liked the idea of learning about skincare and cosmetics as a career. My option was to study for the course in Sydney and commute the four hours' return train trip each day, which would mean a total of thirteen hours. I baulked at the idea, thinking it was all way too hard, and I never enquired if there was an alternate way.I never saw the vision that I could become a business owner and set up my own beauty salon.

If there is something you desperately want to be or do, then don't let anything stop you. There is always a solution or answer to any challenge and quitting on your dreams shouldn't be an option.

If you ask yourself, "If I don't pursue this now, where will I be in five years' time?" the answer will always be you're in the same place, doing the same unfulfilling or boring thing, and nothing would have changed.

The purpose of this book is to help you make good choices and decisions. There are no mistakes in life, and by making better decisions, you're not falling into the trap of living a meaningless life and, therefore, sabotaging your happiness.

My second choice was a career in nursing and becoming a registered nurse, a very worthwhile and fulfilling job and a service to the community.

After applying and being accepted, I lived in the nurses' home to study and do my training for three years. After only twenty months, I quit and walked away from it all. How dumb is that? I only had another sixteen months to go till I finished. I lost my focus and let my dream slip away. And that is something that I have regretted for many years. I guess that's way I'm always learning and interested in health issues even now. Nursing was my life's purpose, and I have used every excuse of why not go back and why it couldn't be possible – too old, not smart enough, married with family, who will look after the children, and don't have the time.

If starting a course, it's always better to finish it, get your qualifications, and keep it in your portfolio. It shows a potential employer that you are capable of finishing something you started.

If you find you absolutely hate the course and it wasn't what you expected, check out if you can change the course.

Check out the fine print before signing up. Maybe they have a cooling-off period or perhaps you may obtain a percentage of a refund.

It's impossible to relive your life again. This is not a dress rehearsal. So really think seriously about your dreams and goals.

There are no correct or incorrect answers to any situation. We all make mistakes. I'm just giving you some guidance that could save you a lot of money, heartache, and regrets.

You will come across obstacles throughout your life, whether they're career, marriage, or something else, so please take into account all your options and facts before you make big decisions.

You want to make sure you are getting all your options and facts from a qualified person who has the authority in that particular subject.

In other words, never listen to the office girl if you want to know how to install a light fitting, you would ask a qualified electrician.

If you are still going to school, then you need to factor in study in your first column.

You will need to work out how many hours of study you will

need to do for each subject. You may need to factor in time frames for lectures, assignments, group sessions, or a part-time job if applicable.

When you are in year ten at school, choose elective subjects that you like and think would be relevant to your choice of career you may undertake.

Personal Goals

Your personal goals can be anything you want. Let your imagination go wild here. Maybe it's to skydive the beach, climb Sydney Harbour Bridge, visit Melbourne for shopping and watch the Melbourne cup horse racing live, learn a new language such as French or Italian, or dine at all the fancy restaurants in every capital city of Australia.

When you've finished your list, beside each one of your goals, mark it as a short-term or long-term goal and state the time frame.

When you have achieved one of your goals, cross it off the list as complete.

Review this list every month. You may need to change your goals because of circumstances which are out of your control.

Dream Goals

Dream goals are achievable if they are realistic enough. For instance, if your dream is to have five billion dollars in your bank account so you would be secure and comfortable for the future, firstly, you need to ask yourself why you need to have that amount of money in the bank. You might say, "I want to buy my own private jet to fly to different holiday locations."

But you could actually hire a jet for that same purpose, and you would have saved a huge amount of money on expenses. You wouldn't need to spend all that money on things you only use occasionally or work as long saving for it.

Perhaps you may want to own a house on one of the Greek islands in the Mediterranean Sea and live there for six months of the year, learn to fly a helicopter, or sail the Whitsundays in your very own yacht. Use your imagination and enjoy dreaming.

Money Goals

When you first start work and receive your first pay, you will most likely say to yourself, "Oh yes, so much money, and I'm going to spend it all on myself."

Did you know that even high-paid earners with executive jobs still find it hard to make ends meet and are living from paycheque to paycheque? And yet I personally know workers on minimal wages who actually retired as millionaires or very wealthy and comfortable. The difference was that the high-paid workers lived way beyond their means, and the lower-paid workers had budgets or plans in place to reach their goals. There is an expression: "She has champagne tastes on beer budget." In other words, the person is spending far more than they earn.

You need to be realistic, so don't leave yourself without any money for a night out with your girlfriends. I have devoted chapter five to money matters, so for now just work out how much money you think you would like to have for a comfortable life.

Contribution Goals

A contribution goal is something that you want to give back to helping others who are less fortunate than you. It could be contributing items such as clothing or tin food to world hunger or sending money to an African village and feeding a family for a whole year.

Or your money could supply good, clean water for the whole village or educate ten girls where education is not valued in their country. You could volunteer your time and services for twelve months in a remote village that's been devastated by an earthquake or hurricane. It could be simply donating tin foods, money, or giving Christmas gifts locally in your community.

There are plenty of opportunities to give to others, free babysitting, walking the neighbour's dog, or doing gardening for your elderly grandparents. You could volunteer your time reading and talking with the elderly at the nursing homes. The possibilities are endless, and you will be amazed how wonderful you will feel by helping someone else.

Health Goals

Do you have a goal that you want to compete in a fun run or a marathon, the Olympics or Paralympics perhaps? Then you already know you need to train hard and dedicate a lot of time into your dream.

Maybe you want to compete as a body builder, and that's going to take a lot of mental and physical strength.

If you want to become healthy, you need to exercise regularly, drink at least eight glasses of water a day, eat good, nutritious food, and get at least seven to eight hours' sound sleep a night, plenty of fresh air and sunshine. You will need to exercise every day and abstain from smoking and drinking alcohol or cut back. Have a good positive attitude and be surrounded by positive, like-minded friends to hang around with.

When you have finished your list and marked on your paper if they are short-term or long-term goals, state also the time frame in which you would like to complete them.

Vision Board

Now that you have your dreams and goals in place, it's time to have a little fun. Purchase a large sheet of cardboard and make a vision board of pictures or quotes of your dream goals that you can look at every day.

It could be a picture of you in a car that you would like to drive and own one day. So go down to your local car yard dealer and find the exact same car model and colour you want. Get one of your friend's or Dad or Mum to take a picture of you sitting in the driver's seat.

Have the photo processed and then stick it on your vision board. Your dream could be to own a Ferrari, yacht, mansion, or a 4WD-you can dream as big as you want.

You can find pictures in brochures and magazines. Travel agencies are excellent for finding pictures of landscapes and hotels, a photo of the Eiffel Tower in Paris or a landscape picture of the Grand Canyon or any of the places you want to visit or have a holiday.

Choose pictures of your dream career, maybe a policewoman or a nurse for instance.

For your health goals, it could be photos of you riding a bike or practicing yoga positions or a picture of a healthy vegetable stir fry dish.

Include pictures of creative activity such as painting, sewing, writing and scrap booking or your favourite movie stars and pop stars. Perhaps one day you may have the opportunity to meet Mr. Dreamy in person by going to one of the music festivals or just by chance in an airport as you walk past or catch the same plane.

Anything is possible. You don't realize how the universe conspires to help you attain your dreams and goals. I have a picture of Channing Tatum on my vision board. Maybe we will meet at Matt Moran's ARIA restaurant near the Opera House in Sydney one day. You just have to keep visualizing the pictures in your thoughts and believe it's possible to attain them.

You can be as creative as you want; it's your artwork. You can write affirmations or quotes if you like. Place your work of art on a wall that you look at every day. Spend a few minutes each morning and before you go to bed visualizing on how great your life will be when you achieve your goals.

Now the next exercise isn't as much fun, but it certainly will keep you on track of your goals. Scheduling in your weekly activities is very important with the intention of staying focused to get your priorities in place for your dreams to manifest.

Have in place a structured timetable schedule allowing you and others to know exactly what and when you are doing something. Block out certain days and times that you need to study or any activity to achieve your goals and don't deviate from this. Then you will have a good system in place. This tells others you do not wish to be disturbed and make it clear that you want them to respect your wishes.

You may, for example, allocate Monday night basketball training between 6.00 p.m. and 7.30 p.m. or Saturday girl's nights out at the movies and Sunday family lunch get-togethers.

You will need to be flexible at times, if you have a big exam coming up or need to spend extra time on a couple of assignments.

You may think that you don't have time to schedule your life, but the truth of the matter is that if you don't, then everything just gets slotted in haphazardly.

Say you have a project that's due in two weeks' time and you have all good intentions of handing in a decent piece of work. Preparation is everything so you think about what you're going to do and then you forget all about it. Time slips away because you work on other things, and no way are you ready to hand in a good project.

You knew that you should have been working on your project for at least thirty minutes each day to get the high quality of work you wanted to hand in to your teacher. The end result is you have run out of time. You goofed, and it's not the work you're happy with. You will need to structure in your time wisely if you want to be successful and learn to say no to other people and distractions. Sometimes you will need to be somewhere that's really important, such as your nan's sixtieth birthday party and all your aunties, uncles, and cousins are travelling from out of state. That's different, but you get the idea of prioritizing, because without structure it's all wishful thinking.

At the beginning of each new year purchase a diary. If you're studying, get one that's especially for students and pencil in your activities.

Here are some suggestions, you can add your own:

- Work
- School
- Family time
- Time with your friends
- Boyfriend time
- Sports activities
- Training time
- Holidays
- Youth church
- Babysitting
- Choir or music practice
- Study time

Once every activity is in your diary, it will be clear what you need to do and can say no to. Problems or challenges occur for almost everyone. The best plans fall apart. That's life. Don't become overwhelmed. It's a fact of life we are all on a roller coaster ride. Life sends you a little curve ball just to check you in, keep you on your toes. It's a lesson for all of us to see how we handle our emotions. We can kick, scream, and throw a tantrum, or we can chill out, find a solution immediately, get help, or just sleep on it till the morning.

You'll be surprised how the answer to your problems sometimes just pops into your head, and then you can take the appropriate action.

I hope you have been taking my suggestions seriously and are having fun at the same time.

All this information can be a bit daunting and seem like a lot of work, but believe me: it will be so worth it when you reach your goals, and that's when you can celebrate. Remember: being mature comes with responsibility, and you will be so glad you have exercised your own rights to make good decisions.

CHAPTER 3

· · · · · · · · · · · · · · · ·

TEMPTING ADDICTIONS

W hen Adam and Eve lived in the Garden of Eden and they were told by God not eat the fruit from the tree of the knowledge of good and evil, they were tempted by Satan, and Eve offered the forbidden apple to Adam, and they both ate the fruit. They instantly were ashamed and tried to cover and hide themselves from God. But you can't hide from God, because that's impossible, and so He banished them from the garden for their disobedience.

We also have temptations in life, and these are either legal or illegal. Doing the wrong thing will always have consequences, whether directly, such as a jail term, or indirectly by guilt or shame brought to yourself, friends, or family.

The temptation addictions I'm referring to are illegal or legal, drugs, alcohol, gambling, and cigarette smoking.

For the majority of teenagers there is many temptations, you will be tempted to smoke your first cigarette as these are easily accessible but many vices are illegal if you are under the age of eighteen years. The government and companies make millions of dollars from the sales and taxes on legal cigarette smoking. Alcohol and gambling provide thousands of jobs, so they will be here to stay. Some adults can't handle temptations and get themselves into trouble by losing their health, job, money, homes, marriages, children, respect, and confidence. Not a pretty scenario, is it? But what you need to know is it's the addiction to substances or temptations in the first place. People use these temptations for a number of reasons but mostly to escape from reality. Life isn't going well for them, and getting high for just a few hours will seem great to deaden the emotional or physical pain. And that's when you're hooked and you become dependent on it.

Alcohol

Aussies have a reputation for being big alcohol drinkers' at most venues or social events. Big alcohol drinkers or alcoholics eventually hide away from the prying eyes of the public in the comfort and privacy of their homes. Behind closed doors they can't be judged by family, friends and neighbours when they lose control of normal day to day functions.

If a person doesn't drink alcohol, he or she is considered to be weird, unsociable, and that person is sometimes bullied by his or her workmates or peers. Most people are sensible and have plans that one person will be allotted the designated car driver for a night out. You need to be careful when buying alcohol drinks or having others buy drinks for you. Drugs can be slipped into your drink when you are not looking. Rohypnol is one type of date rape drug. These drugs often have no colour, smell, taste, so they may go undetected. Sometimes it may be friends of friends who are prank spikers and just want to see what reaction you might have. Unfortunately, these pranksters don't consider that their actions are criminal, constitute an assault, and are harmful. More than likely, it's some undesirable stranger who's lurking about, waiting to spike your drink, so watch out for anybody suspicious hanging around.

After slipping you the drug, they are waiting for you to leave the premises, or they may try and pick you up. The effects of Rohypnol can be effective within thirty minutes of being drugged and can last for several hours. You could feel dizzy or weak. You may have stomach problems or seem drunk and confused even though you haven't been drinking a lot, so you could be a target. Or you may pass out, unable to refuse sex or defend yourself.

You may have blank spots in your memory or never remember anything about the night before when you wake up. I know a beautiful, intelligent young girl who believed her drink was spiked and that she was raped, but she never reported the incident. She was ashamed of herself for allowing this to happen and suffered many months of depression, withdrawing from all social events. Eventually, her family encouraged her to get counselling, and she is now happily married to a wonderful man.

Males can be targeted also. My daughter was a guest at a beach wedding, and the reception was held on the public beach. During the night, her boyfriend wasn't seen, which was strange, as it was relatively early in the evening and he wasn't with the other guys. My daughter and her girlfriends also noticed a couple of guys hanging around them, trying to get too friendly.

Common sense kicked in, and realizing something wasn't quite right, the girls took off in search of my daughter's boyfriend. A short while later, they found my daughter's boyfriend, and he appeared quite drunk and dazed. Now this guy can hold his beer really well, so it all seemed rather suspicious. They all believe he was a victim of his drink being spiked, and the ploy was to have him out of the picture for a while.

We can only speculate what might have happened, and it could have been a different outcome. Now that you are aware of how important it is to be not overly trusting of everyone, this could be vital information to you and your friends.

Even though alcohol is legal, it still can destroy an individual's life and his or her family. When consumed in large amounts daily, alcohol turns a person's everyday capabilities into a battle ground. It's the cause of many arguments, fights, misunderstandings, and marriage breakups.

Many people have fallen under its spell of false confidence and foolish mistakes. There is nothing honourable watching someone drunk, slurring his or her words in a simple conversation while trying to keep his or her balance and eventually falling over. Perhaps you have witnessed someone who gets drunk every day, or maybe you are a binge drinker yourself every weekend when you go out. Unfortunately, it's now very common for girls to drink excessively when they have a night out, and they become loud and obnoxious, and their behaviour is disrespectful.

Alcohol changes a person's personality so he or she does and say things that otherwise may be out of character. The thing you should know about alcohol is it's a depressant and frees up your inhibitions.

A girl who's drunk becomes irresponsible and certainly not too discriminating about whom she has sex with, and most of the time can't even remember the guy. If she continues on this self-destructive pathway, several situations can happen. She could be raped or gang raped. She may become pregnant or contract any of the venereal diseases or HIV/AIDS from some undesirable character. She may even be beaten up, robbed, and left to defend for herself in the gutter or choke on her own vomit.

All the drinking of cans of beer, wine, or spirits you consumed and happily enjoyed takes a toll on your liver, and the side effects of getting drunk aren't all that appealing. Before you know it, your speech is slurred and you can't stand up unaided. The room will feel like it's spinning, you'll be seeing double, and you will be groaning with pain as your stomach muscles are contracting whilst vomiting. Your dry mouth and sense of taste and smell resembles rotting food.

Having a hangover isn't a great experience. All you want to do is lie down on your bed in complete darkness and silence, as your head will be thumping with pain.

One wonders how people can say they had a great time when most can't remember a thing that happened. How do I know this? Well, from experience on more than a few occasions when I have looked and felt like something the cat dragged in. These days, I have an alcoholic drink on the odd occasion, and even then it is just a couple of drinks at Christmas time. Some people are happy drunks, others get depressed and angry or want to argue and pick fights. Continually getting drunk and on the path of self-destruction then, eventually it will be harder for you to concentrate in your work, studies, or school work.

Therefore, your performance and memory will be poor, with falling grades resulting in poor exam results, reprimands, suspension, or even unemployment, as there are always consequences. No one escapes the clutches of this demon, you think you have it all under control, but be careful. It silently becomes addictive. Instant dismissal is the right of every employer who finds an employee on the job who has been drinking alcohol. And rightfully so, because you could be risking yourself and other workers to danger using company equipment and machinery.

Family breakdowns are a common occurrence, with respect and trust violated, especially if violence is involved.

A tarnished reputation is the cause of loss of friends, but hopefully, you will have one or two sincere friends who will stick by you. Unfortunately, your friends' parents may forbid you to hang around their children and home. Or perhaps you have been misled by friends, and they are the ones leading you down a path of destruction. An if you've been sacked from employment, then all your wonderful plans for that trip to Paris or the ownership of the shiny, red convertible, you can kiss these dreams goodbye.

If you don't seek help, it could eventually lead to alcoholism, poor health, or other temptations, such as using illegal drugs, prostitution, or stealing. Take a good hard look where you live, in the city or the country, and you will most likely see a pattern unfolding. Young people with no jobs, not enough money, bored out of their minds because there's nothing to do but hang around the parks or shopping malls. If you are in this jobless situation, my advice is to seek all the learning you can, take all the relevant training to find employment, and volunteer your time to learn.

When I was seeking employment, I volunteered for almost twelve months to learning on the job training. And that job led me to employment for twenty-four years in paid employment in the health industry.

Education is one of the most beneficial things you can get in your life. It gives you self-confidence and a purpose for living and eventually leads to employment. Don't ever be discouraged if you don't find work at first, the skills that you have obtained will make you an asset for future employers. While we still have all vices for self-destruction, the difference today is that most of us have better living conditions with lawful protection. We have the opportunity to obtain-higher education, be respected, and treated equally, and the prospect of becoming wealthy if we so choose. Make your voice count in constructive ways to those in higher power in government if you believe that you are being wrongly disadvantaged by social injustice.

Look, there is nothing wrong with enjoying an alcoholic drink as long as you can handle the strong beverage and provided you are the legal age of eighteen years old. I hear that underage drinking is becoming quite rampant in teens and even as young as twelve year olds.

Underage Teen Drinking
Photo @ Josep Curto / Dreamtime.com

Your brain and your body are not equipped to handle all those chemicals, and you're really setting yourself up for a toxic liver.

If you study nutrition, you will read that alcohol not only affects your health now but also any unborn children you could have in the future.

The effects of alcohol consumed not only by the mother but also by the father are well documented in unborn children, even causing mental retardation. I'm sure most of you have been educated about drink driving, and I hope you wouldn't get behind the wheel if you had been drinking. For a P plate driver, it is zero tolerance for alcohol. Get caught and it will be driver's license disqualification. You can still be fined by law if you're riding a push bike while intoxicated.

Most recently there has been a lot of talk about the tragic deaths of two teenagers, Thomas Kelly and Daniel Christie in Kings Cross, Sydney, New South Wales. Each of these young men were enjoying nights out with their friends on different Saturday nights, when they were "king hit" (punched in the head from behind) by complete strangers.

This behaviour destroys families, the victim's as well as the attacker's, leaving an emptiness in the family unit. Another young man, Matthew Domio, thirty years old, was highly intoxicated when he king hit his own father, Dario Domio, during an argument Dario was rushed to hospital, unconscious and with bleeding on his brain. He died two days later.

The state government now has a mandatory eight years jail sentence for offenders who carry out an assault that causes death while intoxicated.

Still think it's worth getting blotto on a night out on the town? With the arguments, punch-up fights, drink glasses broken and smashed into your face. Now, thankfully, most hotel patrons drink from plastic drinking cups.

Gambling

There's one famous horse race that Australians love to celebrate, the Melbourne Cup, held at Flemington Race Course Victoria on the second Tuesday in November. The day offers a full day's horse racing, betting, and fashions on the field, with scrumptious dining and champagne flowing. The negative side of horse racing is the cruelty to the horses, with some horses dying after racing incurred from internal bleeding. My interest and excitement is observing the stunning and creative hats and fascinators on race day, as I dabble in millinery work, as a hobby.

The punters can choose fine dining in the restaurants or eat a picnic lunch in the car park, swilling a can of beer while wearing a fascinator or hat. Those who don't have a bet on any horse race during the year will make an exception on this day, even if they enter the sweeps at work. On the same week, the lotto will always have a first division prize of a few million dollars AUD at least.

You can have a bet on almost anything, card games, poker machines, dog racing, football, lottery tickets, cricket, etc. The Australian government has announced the discontinuation of greyhound dog racing by July 2017 but I believe they have reversed their decision. All forms of gambling can be addictive, especially poker machines. When you get the ideal combination of winning symbols in one line or more, then you have won a prize. With a win, all the coloured lights flash, music rings out on the poker machine, and you start getting excited. Depending on how much money you gamble, the machine will work out how much money you will receive. Those persons who tell you they won five hundred dollars on the pokies probably actually lost more money over the last couple of weeks whilst they were playing the machines.

When you reach a point when you're gambling and start chasing your money, then it's time to walk away from the machine. You keep losing your money but keep hoping that if you place more money in the slot machine, then next time you press the button, you're going to hit the jackpot and win your money back. I know personally of one person putting all his fortnightly wages and three weeks' holiday pay in the pokies and losing all the money in one night.

And the husband one of my school friend's, unknown to his wife, put their home up as collateral to the bank and gambled it all and lost the family home over a period of three years.

Gambling can be okay on the odd bet, but be mindful of the dangers, and gamble money you are prepared to lose.

These days there are a lot more women gambling. They work and have their own money. Most are single, widowed or divorced, and independent. Some are married and play bingo or the pokies while their husbands are out working.A woman can go into a club and not even be noticed by others, sitting playing a poker machine all night as they might play a few machines. They might be loners, and this is how they enjoy their social lives, surrounding themselves with the noises of machines and people.

Prescription Drugs

Prescription drugs are legal, but when they are abused and misused by the patient, they can be addictive. Example are Valium, Serepax, Mogadon, and Diazepam, or barbiturates found in sleeping pills and strong pain killers, synthetic derivates of narcotic analgesics.

Illegal Drugs

Illegal drugs are not manufactured under strict standards and guidelines in accordance to the law. The buyer doesn't know if the lab has used a cheaper poison to dilute the drug.

Side effects include - possible permanent damage to your brain, liver, kidneys and heart as well as confusion, anxiety, paranoia, panic attacks, nausea, shaking, headache, schizophrenic and psychotic behaviour, hostile and aggressive behaviour, violence, and possible permanent mental illness.

Being caught using or selling drugs is a serious crime, and a jail term is probable. A user has the risk of AIDS/HIV if sharing hypodermic needles.

Mental health problems and the risk of an overdose can occur. Have you ever watched someone who is under the influence of illicit drugs? Not a pretty sight. You can't believe that a once very attractive girl now has a very thin build, sallow skin, pimples on the face, and sunken eyes. Her personality can be extremely agitated or jittery, and she sometimes talks nonstop to anyone listening or becomes withdrawn from family.

I'm sure you have been taught not to take illegal drugs, but of course, you're faced with peer pressure from others to give them a try. Users tell you it won't harm you, it will just give you a buzz, and you will feel like you can do anything, even fly. If you're curious to know what it's like, you're probably going to be tempted to try drugs at the next party you attend.

Well, Saturday night is here, and you have handed over your cash for a little packet of white powder or a bong. Did you even think that white powder or smoke could be laced with cheap, inferior ingredients, a lethal cocktail that could cause serious harm or even death? It does happen; there have been tragic deaths of first - time users.

Did it occur to you that one in a hundred who gets caught in possession of illegal drugs will be placed before the courts? Think seriously about the friends and the acquaintances you're hanging around with; some may just be placing you in a dangerous snare. It's good to have fun, but make sure that fun is not destructive to yourself and others or possessions.

Cigarettes

People always seemed to have that cool look about them whenever they smoked cigarettes. I've watched people do the drawback or flick the ash off the end of the smoke and thought how cool they looked.

I thought nothing about the dangers of cigarette smoking with its harmful ingredients in each cigarette. After all, most everyone has tried smoking. Cigarette smoking was encouraged and rationed to our Anzacs during World War 1 and World War 2, and even British Prime Minister Sir Winston Churchill's trade mark was smoking a fat cigar. The famous Marlene Dietrich smoked little cigars on and off the screen. Most actors and actresses were often pictured with a cigarette in their mouth or hand. It became an accepted part of the social culture and was even heavily advertised on television commercials and billboard sporting fixtures.

The beginning of this century was a turning point and billboard and media advertising stopped and now cigarette companies display warnings of smoking on cigarette packets. But, unfortunately, this didn't help to deter young adolescents from smoking and only encouraged more young girls to start smoking. The two hundred harmful ingredients, many of which are addictive, are precursors to most of the health problems today, such as respiratory and heart disease, and cancer.

Perhaps the majority of adolescent girls will try one of these vices at least once, because of curiosity, peer pressure, illegality, and because they want to seem cool and look and feel grown-up.

They're at an age where they're rebelling against all of society. They want to try things out, they don't want to be told what to do, and they feel they want to make their own mistakes.

Yes, that's all well and good, and I completely understand-believe me: I do.

I just don't want you to make decisions that don't align with your true beliefs or nature.

Remember the dreams and goals that you want desperately to achieve that you wrote down on your vision board, I hope you do fulfil each and every one of them.

Most of you have heard of the Bali Nine, who were tempted into a false hope of making easy money on a trip to Bali, Indonesia, just by being drug mules and collecting five thousand dollars is a lot of easy cash for anybody. But they were caught and convicted of drug trafficking and possession of illegal drugs in the Bali airport. Six men and one women are now serving life sentences in a filthy Bali prison, and the two drug leaders have already been executed. Mess with the wrong people in a foreign country whose drug laws are extremely harsh and you are setting yourself up for failure and misery. Either way, using or selling illegal drugs will stuff your life up and be one downward-spiralling journey of destruction.

Help is available for all temptation traps, alcoholics, drug users, drug suppliers, sex addicts, and gamblers if you want it. No one should judge. People should congratulate you for being honest with yourself and coming forward asking for help. Prevention of these temptation traps is better than the cure and less painful. Making wise choices and not getting hooked in the first place is a sign of maturity.

I remember having a conversation with a patient, and he gave this advice to all of his children as they were walking out the door for a night out on the town. "Don't do anything that would bring disgrace to the family name and have a good time." I have never forgotten his wise words, so as a suggestion, repeat them every time you go for a night out.

My wish for you is to have good, clean fun and friends who watch out for each other.

CHAPTER 4

* * * * * * * * * * * * * * * *

UNZIP YOUR FASHION STYLE

H ave you ever looked at your wardrobe and said, "I can't find a thing to wear," or "My clothes look disgusting on me"? When you know and understand your style personality and buy the appropriate clothes, there will be no need to say these words ever again. Learning what clothing suits you for your figure, lifestyle, personality, and budget is the first step. Most of you will be still at school or studying and not earning a lot of money. But with limited incomes, you can still look like a million dollars or a fashion queen. It's just knowing the right colour and style for that dramatic effect and mix and matching clothes.

Your style personality can be dramatic, creative, natural, romantic, classic, city chic, gothic, or country. You will be more comfortable in any outfit, whatever the occasion, knowing your personality style. Learning how to accessorize and mix and match pieces of clothing will give you an array of different looks. Applying tricks and techniques on how to dress will have you from drab or ordinary to looking stunning or fabulous. When you look unique with your own style of clothing, this will boost your self-confidence and self-esteem. You want people to notice the total effect of you and not just comment on the colour of your outfit.

Clothes should be appropriately styled for your age and

personality, flatter your body type and proportions, and complement your colouring. In your early teens, you will notice your body shape changing. Your breasts will develop fully, and your waistline will be more defined. Where possible, when you start wearing bras, have one professionally fitted by a trained undergarment specialist at a department store or one of the specialty shops. This will be a lifelong valuable lesson on how wearing the right bra and correct size with your outfit can make the most of your figure. At least once a year, get fitted professionally as your sizing may vary and try on a range of styles from different brands, some cuts will fit you better than others.

Most girls want to flaunt their breasts and may choose a padded, uplifting bra and low-cut, revealing outfits that will cause shock or surprise to others. Don't be in any hurry to grow-up by looking older; you may actually just look silly and vulgar. Following the latest clothing, fashion trends, regardless of whether they suit you or not, often can be a big rip-off in regards to your money and appearance. You might not even be interested in fashion shopping or personal grooming, but with some new positive ideas, this will influence how others see and treat you.

Teenage fashion Style
Photo @ Kristina Afanasyeva /Dreamtime.com

Before starting or even thinking about changing your wardrobe, you need to be comfortable with your body image. This means accepting your body shape right now and making the most of your good assets and playing down any ones you're not comfortable with. When you have a free day, pull out all your clothes from your wardrobe and divide them into three piles.

The first pile is all your favourite clothing, a second pile for the op shop or to sell on eBay, and the last pile for clothes you like but never seem to wear. Try your clothes on and check if they fit correctly. If they don't, place them in your second pile. Dress in a number of outfits and look objectively at your body shape. Even the top models and celebrities have hang-ups, so please don't beat yourself up too much.

Although reality TV celebrity Kim Kardashians is noted for her well-proportioned figure and is worth millions of dollars, making her one of the highest-paid reality stars today. It's all about her own self-confidence. Kim doesn't look to others for opinions of herself, and it's about her own perception of herself. Now, of course, she has lost those kilos and has even published a book on how she did it, still raking in more wealth.

Understandably, the real beauty is what's inside you. This- is the authentic you. Accepting your body shape is accepting yourself. If you are a big girl and you feel healthy, then that's better than being slim and feeling lousy. Having a bad attitude and coming across as grumpy, arrogant, angry, and bitter means no one will really like you, even if you are wearing the latest fashion. Being pleasant, well-mannered, and happy towards others while wearing something stylish and simple, will cause people to naturally gravitate towards you. If you do believe you are a plain Jane or frumpy Susan, I'll reveal the secrets so you can dress amazingly, comfortable and confident with your appearance.

If you feel you need to lose weight, then start moving more and eating less foods that contain white sugar or white flour ingredients. Start noticing all the hidden ingredients and calories in the foods and drinks you consume. Being mindful of what you eat, the kilos should start coming off, and you will start losing centimetres, and clothes will start to become baggy. Losing weight will be beneficial to your health if you are overweight, and further reading is available in chapter 7, "Diet, Health, and Fitness."

Choosing Your Style Personality

It is important that clothes do fit in with your lifestyle, whether it's for work, school, or leisure. Also your clothes should fit the occasion. You wouldn't wear a cocktail dress to a barbeque, for instance.

I remember as a teenager wearing a lovely, brightly orange-coloured dress with small heels and stockings to a car racing event at Oran Park in Sydney. At the time, I realized I must have looked stupid, standing up all day when what would have been more appropriate and comfortable wearing a pair of jeans, top, and joggers. So if some guy asks you on a date, find out exactly where you're going and what's the occasion so you don't stand out looking like a pimple on an elephant's backside.

Choosing the Right Colours for You

This can be a little tricky, because you may love a certain colour, but it doesn't suit your colouring. So what you do is keep the colour you love away from your facial features. Wear your favourite colour in a skirt or pair of pants, for instance. I have been to a couple of personal stylist workshops and learnt how wearing different colours make you feel and what impression you give others, firstly knowing what the psychology of colours mean and, secondly, how certain colours can make your face light up and your eye colour more enhanced.

For an exercise, I want you to purchase two pieces of cotton material, enough to drape over your shoulders and around your neck. One piece will be a brilliant white and the other a cream colour. Sit in front of a bathroom mirror and compare each coloured piece one at a time. You should have bare-faced skin, so no makeup, and look closely at your reflection in the mirror.

Is your face more illuminated, smoother, fresher with the white piece of cloth or the cream one? If you are unsure, ask for the opinion of another person, such as your mum, to give you an unbiased point of view. As a general rule, usually blonde-coloured hair is better with cream or warmer tones, and dark-haired persons look good in white or cooler tones.

What you want is that you stand out more than the colour you're wearing. When you start wearing different colours, take notice of your emotions. How do you feel? Are- you more confident, sexier, brighter, and happier when you're wearing certain colours in your colour pallet? Then you're wearing the right colour in your colour pallet, and you will look and feel a million dollars.

Blondes with Blue, Grey, or Green Eyes and Light Skin

Your ideal colours are the following

- cream, ivory
- light or medium grey
- peacock, turquoise, light teal blue
- pastel or dusty pink
- stone, taupe
- apple green or mint
- light navy, violet
- apricot

Of course if you have warm skin tones you could wear gold, lemon, yellow-green, watermelon, salmon, or buttermilk colours.

If you have cool skin undertones, your colours could include pink, rose, lavender, bluebell colours.

Remember if you love a certain colour, but it's not your most flattering look, then wear the colour away from your face by diffusing it with a beautiful scarf or a junky piece of coloured choker in your colour pallet.

Red Heads

Your ideal colours with a warm skin undertone include the following

- cream
- brown
- charcoal
- gold
- dark green
- teal or aqua
- lavender
- navy
- apricot

- purple
- lime
- bronze

Your ideal colour with a cool skin undertone are any of these

- yellow green
- moss
- peach
- coral pink
- salmon
- buttermilk
- lemon
- watermelon

Dark Brown, Black Hair, Dark Eyes, Eyebrows, and Lashes

Your ideal colours are the following

- teal
- dark-navy
- blue-red
- scarlet
- purple
- burgundy
- chocolate
- taupe
- soft white
- charcoal
- lime
- aubergine
- emerald green

Your ideal colours with a warm skin undertone are salmon, mustard, mahogany, rust, pumpkin, olive, light pewter, forest green, and camel.

Your ideal colours with a cool skin undertone are

fuchsia, teal, plum, pure white, pale blue, periwinkle, black, and violet.

The Psychology of Colours

Colours can communicate non-verbal messages

- Soft and light colours make you appear friendly.
- **Red** is energizing and can make you feel self-assured.
- Wearing all over **black** gives the impression of authority.
- **Brown** denotes a friendly but serious attitude.
- **Beige** is non-threatening and you are approachable.
- **Dark blue** conveys trust and order and light blue is feminine and softer.
- **Pink** is girly and will lift any complexion when you're feeling off colour.
- **Purple** suggests royalty.
- **Green** is calming and shows creativity and imagination.
- **Black** lacks imagination.

Colour Combinations

If you use only one colour for the entire outfit, such as a black dress and stockings, this will give the appearance of height. Different colours for a jacket, pants and top will give the illusion of reducing height.

A jacket, skirt, or pants in one colour and a top in another colour is a great combo for everybody.

If you wish to give the illusion of being slimmer, use dark colours, and where you wish to emphasize your appearance, use a lighter colour. Brighter colours worn near the face will draw attention away from problem areas such as bigger thighs, hips, or stomach. A dark top with a light pair of pants will give the impression of slimmer top and wider hips. A light top and darker bottoms will give the impression of wider shoulders and narrower hips. Black has always been the most popular colour for slimmer appearances, but it can look very draining if it's not your colour. You could also use navy, brown, pine, purple, and charcoal colours that will make you look slimmer.

Dressing for Your Age and Body Shape

There is nothing more worrying for a parent than seeing their thirteen - year old daughter dressing like an eighteen year old. The reason is that your appearance can be sending the wrong message when you look older than your real age. You may be approached by older boys and may not have the maturity to deal with situations that may place you in extreme danger. I've noticed young girls no more than fifteen - years old, out in the shopping malls in the daytime wearing full makeup with thick, black eyeliner and mascara.

Young skins should look fresh and natural without caked-on makeup. More appropriately, you could wear tinted moisturizer. There is plenty of time to apply full makeup every day to enhance your appearance when you're older. Of course, on special occasions or if you're a performer on stage with dancing concerts or eisteddfods, it's essential to wear makeup as part of your costume.

Dressing for your body shape shouldn't be too hard, but unfortunately, a lot of girls get this wrong. I find young girls flaunting their boobs with low-cut cut tops and exposing the cheeks of their bums with short shorts extremely degrading for a girl. There is nothing left to the imagination with breasts showing or short, tight skirts with glimpses of panties when girls bend over or sit down.

Look, I am no prude by any means. It's just that you are really attracting guys who are likely to take advantage of you. This is nothing new. Women have been flaunting themselves, making themselves sexually attractive to the opposite sex since time began. Any girl dressing smartly and covering her private parts appropriately, will be treated with respect by others. You have heard the saying that a picture paints a thousand words, and so my tip is to cover up and give the world a bit of a tease. I love this powerful message, so read the next words carefully and remember them.

The late famous boxer Muhammad Ali said these words to his daughters when they arrived at his home wearing clothes that were not modest.

Here is the story as told by one of his daughters:

> When we finally arrived, the chauffeur escorted my younger sister, Laila, and me up to my father's suite. As usual, he was hiding behind the door, waiting to scare us. We exchanged many hugs and kisses as we could possibly give in one day.
>
> My father took a good look at us. Then he sat me down on his lap and said something that I will never forget. He looked me straight in the eyes and said, "Hana, everything that God made valuable in the world is covered and hard to get to. Where do you find diamonds? Deep down in the ground, covered and protected. Where do you find pearls? Deep down at the bottom of the ocean, covered up and protected in a beautiful shell. Where do you find gold? Way down in the mine, covered over with layers and layers of rock. You've got to work hard to get to them.
>
> He looked at me with serious eyes.
>
> "Your body is sacred. You're far more precious than diamonds and pearls, and you should be covered

too." (Hana Ali, *"More Than a Hero: Muhammad Ali's Life Lessons through His Daughter's Eyes)"*

Larger Persons and the Tall, Skinny Ones

Larger persons can look very stylish by wearing plain, dark colours and clothes fitted not too tightly or too baggy. Just by wearing a long, wide scarf or long strands of beads will elongate the look.

Wearing a plain, dark-coloured, single-breasted long jacket or cardigan with decorative edging also gives slimming effect. A long-strapped shoulder bag (make sure it's not a small one) draped over the shoulder looks good.

If you are tall and skinny, then you can wear horizontal stripes and different colour blocks and whatever plain or patterned top or blouse you want to wear. You pretty much can enjoy wearing almost anything, although finding clothes that are long enough in the pant legs is a challenge.

I guess that's why it's good to know a good dressmaker or learn to do alterations yourself. The whole idea is to be selective and comfortable with the clothes you are wearing and not to be somebody else you wish to be.

I hope that you have enjoyed reading this chapter, and if you implement some of these suggestions, then you are setting yourself up for success. Successful dressing is getting more value for your money by saving money in buying clothes that look good with the right colours to show your best features.

Buying jeans that fit good will vary with different brands, so shop around and try on before you buy. The better quality the jeans, the longer they'll last, but make sure they're slightly uncomfortable when you buy, as they stretch. As you are growing rapidly, it will be more economical to purchase a cheaper pair of jeans. Adding some salt to your washing machine helps to sustain the dye, which will always have your jeans looking good.

CHAPTER 5

BE A MONEY MAGNET

Wouldn't it be great if you rubbed that magic bottle and out jumped your personal genie, granting you three wishes? I could predict that one of your wishes would be a never-ending stream of money. But we all know that's never going to happen, that's just fantasy. You could possibly win the money, even rob a bank and inherit the money, but you will eventually need more money unless you follow a few strategies.

No matter how much you earn, if your out flows are more than your income, you'll soon be in the red or, in other words, in debt. Now all debt isn't bad. For instance, if you borrow money for a loan to buy a house to live in, that's called a positive debt, because you have to live somewhere and you may as well be paying off your own home and one day own it. If you're paying rent for your housing, you will be paying your landlord, and he or she will be building up his or her own wealth. Going into debt for a new stereo that you purchased on your credit card, because the item will depreciate (in other words, lose value), that's a negative debt.

When you first start work and get your first pay, you'll probably blow all your money on shoes and clothes. And it doesn't matter how much you earn, you probably will spend it all and live from one pay week to the next pay week. And the banks and credit unions will allow you to have a credit card, and this makes it all the more exciting for you, because now you can purchase more stuff.

Credit cards are good if you know how to use them, and that is, every time you get your credit card statement, pay the balance off completely. You must always remember the bank is giving you their money so you can buy goods and services. The credit is a loan, but you still have to pay it back. You need to pay back the money to the bank.

It's so easy to get into debt if you have a credit card, so my advice is to only use it for emergencies. If you know you aren't responsible or disciplined enough to have a credit card, then learn to live without one.

A better option is to own a debit card linked to your savings account, and that way you are purchasing your goods or services with your own money, not the banks. You can only buy goods and services with the money that you have in your savings account. This will provide you with a safety net, because if you try to purchase anything and the card is declined, there probably isn't enough money in your savings account for the purchase.

Learning to manage your money is the secret to wealth. Either cut down on your spending or earn more money.

So how does it all work that you have more money saved?

Like I said, when you first start work you want to buy, buy, buy. It's like Christmas all at once. But like the quote says, "Only a fool parts with all his or her money." By the end of the financial year when you receive your group certificate from your employer, it will tell you how much you earned, and I can guarantee you will ask, "Where did all the money go that I earnt?"

Most companies or businesses have electronic banking arranged in place for their employees. Setting up a bank account in your name is easy, so your wages or pay goes directly into your bank account from your employer.

Next, open another account that's secondary from the first one and make a promise to yourself to make no withdrawals of money until you have reached ten thousand dollars. Save 10 percent of your earnings into this account and watch it grow. This is your investment account. Make sure you're-earning bank interest, and when you have built up your first thousand dollars, you can buy shares in a company or place the money into a term-deposit account, somewhere it is making higher interest. You won't even miss this money, and you will learn to live off the money in your original account.

I have a Christmas club account that gives me money for my holidays as well. You could open up one account especially for buying your first car. The more money you save in the account, the quicker you will achieve your goals. The more money you save, the less money you will need to borrow from the bank and the less interest you will pay back. And this is what it means to have the money working for you and you not working for the bank.

Another option is, when you first start work, you can have the choice of saving some of your own money before tax and adding a certain amount to your superannuation fund, a salary sacrifice. You probably think, well, that's a long, long way off, but if you start early when you're young, you will have a nice amount saved by the time you wish to retire. Your employer also contributes money into your superfund, and the amount depends how much you earn. Also check out the different superannuation funds as they will have different accounting fee charges. When it's time to retire, you may get quite a shock at how much you actually end up with and how much of your money is in your fund manager's pocket.

Most superfunds allow you to move your money around on their websites into different configurations each week as long as they add up to a total of 100 percent. For example, you could have 40 percent of your money in Australia shares, 20 percent in overseas shares, 20 percent in property, 10 percent in cash, and 10 percent in bonds.

Another way to save is to have personal life insurance. You can take out a policy and save money and accumulate wealth by compounding interest into your account. It's never too early to talk to a financial advisor, but always make sure they haven't a vested interest in the products they are trying to sell you or sign you up for.

Make sure you don't get conned into some get-rich quick scheme. If it sounds too good to be true, it probably is. People have been fooled through greed into parting with their good, hard-earned cash into high-risky investments and have lost all the money. Playing it safe with minimal risk is a wise decision if you aren't confident or if you're unsure of the money market.

Car Loans

There's plenty of sharks out there from all walks of life, but watch out for car dealers who will try and persuade you into something you don't really need or want to buy. Buying your first car is an exciting time, and hopefully you have saved up all the money or a good deposit to purchase it.

Remember: the more money you save, the less you need to borrow from the banks. Also, when buying your first car, consider taking a mechanically minded relative or friend with you. You may have stars in your eyes when you look at that shiny, red car that looks fantastic. But consider how many kilometres it has on the clock. Check out the body work and the mechanics. How old is it? Are spare parts still available? Has it been serviced regularly? And don't be conned into the salesman's trick by telling you somebody else is really interested in this car.

Other things to consider are the costs of registration, car insurance, car services, and maintenance. You saved up the money for your car, and you certainly don't want a lemon, so I would advise you having a NRMA roadworthy check. Make sure no money is owing on the vehicle by a finance company. Buying from a car dealer is a safe option, but beware of private sales - they can be risky. You don't want Ostrich Finance Company coming to repossess your car after you bought it and added a new stereo system or mag wheels.

Dream RX7 Sports Car
Photo @ Brian Sullivan/ Dreamtime.com

And make sure before you drive your newly purchased car out of the car yard that you have an insurance cover note from an insurance company of your choosing. If you're under twenty–five years old, car insurance is very expensive, so factor in this expense well ahead of time.

The cover note lasts for thirty days, after which they will send you the full amount owing on your insurance policy. It can easily happen with all the excitement of buying your car that you forget-to get car insurance, and it would be most unfortunate and costly to have an accident. This happened to a young girl who picked up her new car and clipped the back of my daughter's car on a round - about as she was driving it home.

Before you even start looking to purchase a car, and you intend to use finance, check out all your options first. Car finance companies, banks, and credit unions offer different interest rates and just 1 percent difference can save you hundreds of dollars.

Also, check the time frame of the loan. You should aim to pay the loan off as quickly as possible. The quicker you erase the debt, the quicker there's more money in your pocket. The one advantage of your car loan, providing both parties keep the agreement of the contract, is you will have a good credit rating. This will help when you want to purchase a home or even a business sometime in the near future.

But if you default on the contract by falling behind in your car repayments on the due date or can't pay the loan back, it's possible that any loans that you apply for in the future may be declined. This is what's known as a bad debt, and you will have a bad credit rating. So make sure you do your sums honestly and can really afford your new car. If you can't, then wait a little longer and save up more money.

Another shiny new car will be waiting for you and possibly a better one. I always think setbacks happen for a reason. Also consider the time of month or year in purchasing a car. Most car dealers offer better deals towards the end of each month or before the end of the financial year. Try negotiating for a lower price or a few freebies like window tinting or free air conditioning. You will have nothing to lose and everything to gain.

Home Loans

As I have already said, a home loan is a good debt, it forces you to save your money to make weekly repayments. And when the interest rates are low, this is an excellent time to buy, but again, do your sums first, as renting maybe the better option. If you lose your job, fall pregnant, become chronically ill or involved in bad accident and you can't work for some time, this will be added stress that you don't need right now.

If you can't afford the repayments the bank will force you to sell your home to get their money back, and they won't care how much your home is sold for. If at any time you can't afford the house payment, talk with your finance manager as soon as possible so other arrangements can be made. When you are working, it's a good idea to have income protection insurance just in case you are off work for several months through being retrenched, sickness, or injury.

You can even claim your payments back on your yearly income tax claim. Consider all possibilities so you can plan ahead. If the worst-case scenario happens, you will be well prepared and have peace of mind. Perhaps you may even have the opportunity to further your career and work overseas for two years with a huge pay increase to your current income, giving you more time to save money for the deposit on your unit or home if you choose to come back to Australia.

If you purchase way beyond your financial means, you're going to be in a lot of stress and heartache in the future. Remember: this is having champagne tastes on beer budget. Just come down to earth and stay grounded. There is no need to keep up appearances. It's advisable to have at least six months of your current income sitting in the bank for emergencies as you can never be certain of the future. Read the small print of your home loan before you sign any papers, and it's a good idea to take your contract to a solicitor to check if there are any discrepancies. If, for example, you should become a big lotto winner and you choose to pay the loan out right, first check to see if you will incur any penalties, because it may cost you thousands to get out of the original loan.

And if you take only one piece of advice from this chapter on money, let it be this next sentence.

Women should always maintain their financial independence. And the best way is, of course, is to have complete control of your own money and have your own bank account. If you and your partner decide to jointly purchase a home together, don't have a joint banking account where all the money you earn and all your partner's money is pooled together. Don't allow your partner to set the account up where he allows you no money of your own to spend. Have a separate account where an agreed amount of money you earn is solely for your enjoyment.

You don't want to have to account for everything you spend, like having your hair coloured or styled at the hair salon. Be very wary of this arrangement of pooling all your money in together, as someone like this could be controlling you. In theory, it all sounds great: the more money you have for repayments, the quicker the loan is drawn down, saving you money and years. But what a miserable existence to have to justify every little thing you purchase. So keep your independence.

Investing Your Money

There is no reason why women can't be become more business savvy and learn how to invest in the stock market or purchase real estate, not necessary houses, but warehouses or car parking spaces. Education and knowledge should be valued. It is available to all women, and your superfund offers seminars to help you prosper financially. So take advantage of the learning skills offered that will impact your life for the better, with more confidence and the ability to earn more money.

I pray that one day all girls and women living in disadvantaged countries will be able to attend school without the threat of violence and become independent. Gone are the days when women needed marriage certificates to buy real estate and cars. We are capable of being our own bosses or the CEOs of companies. You can earn good money and, with wise investments, be financially secure.

Girls I wish you good luck and prosperity.

Taxable Income

There's a saying: "There are two things in life that are guaranteed, death and taxes." If you work, you will need to pay tax on your gross earnings, and what's left is your net earnings. The tax is calculated on how much you earn from your employer, and this is allocated to the government taxation office.

I like to refer to the tax fund back as my change back from the government. At the end of the financial year, June 30, you will need to fill out and lodge an income tax form. On the form, you state your taxable income and expenses in relationship to your job and other sundries.

You will be required to either obtain a personal or business tax information package for guidance, and you need to keep all your receipts as proof of your business activity or outgoings. If it all seems too daunting, for a small fee you can have your yearly tax processed by a tax agent who will lodge the form to the tax office for you. Once you pay the fee, you will hopefully have a good refund cheque from the taxation office. It's yours to spend or save.

Hopefully I have enlightened you on some of the pros and cons in the world of finance. Money, if used wisely, can give you a comfortable life for yourself and others, or it can be a curse when hoarded, and you become a miserable miser. Remember: money doesn't buy happiness, but it sure makes a lifestyle comfortable.

CHAPTER 6

* * * * * * * * * * * * * * * *

FRIENDS, LOVE, AND CONTRACEPTION

Without friends and socializing, life will be pretty mundane, so organizing time with friends is a worthwhile investment. Girls certainly know how to have a good time, whether it's spending a night out on the town or having a girl's fun night in. Just lounging around in your PJs, watching videos, munching on chocolate and snacks with your friends is all fun. Life can be lonely and miserable if you don't have any friends. Having no friends erodes your self-confidence and self-esteem, which can be unhealthy and confronting. The best way to start making friends, is to smile a lot and appear friendly. If you're extremely shy, then you could join in the conversation by listening. Many people forget that listening is part of conversation too.

My suggestion is to know what's making the news, sports news, celebrities, or who's on top of the music charts and what the latest fashion is. Practice saying out load in front of the mirror at home a conversation that you might have with someone. There are also many groups to join at school, such as the debating team or activities outside, such as sports and drama groups, which will help boost your confidence.

It you have cousins around the same age, hook up with them and go see a movie or watch a basketball game together.

Boyfriends

As you enter adolescence, you will be probably become more interested in boys. If you are a homosexual and attracted to the same sex, then you are called a lesbian. It doesn't matter what your preference of sex is; you will still feel the same intense sensual emotions. Once there is mutual attraction, it's not long before couples are holding hands, cuddling, and kissing. A lot of times couples will spend the majority of their time exclusively together and neglect to spend time with their other friends. This isn't a good idea, because your friends will feel lonely and cheated, realizing that you're under valuing the relationship you have together. You might lose a really good friend, and what if your boyfriend is a real jerk and you dump him (hopefully you do in that case)? I would encourage you to introduce your new friend to your other friends as it's always better to obtain an honest second opinion. Your old friends will let you know if the guy you're dating is someone worthy enough for you. Include everyone in some outings, or if that's not possible, make the extra effort to spend time alone with your old friends.

Romantic Couple
Photo @ Ruslan 1117/Dreamtime.com

Marriage

If you have found that special someone to love and you both want to make a commitment, then you will need to plan for the future. If you both have dreams of going to university, then ideally you will have thought of some strategies to make it work. There is no reason your goals can't be achieved, but you will both need to focus on your end goals.

Statistically, most teenage marriages often end in divorce, because one or both realize later they have grown apart or feel they have missed out on the fun of youth. Most teens aren't mature enough for a lifetime commitment, and one in three marriages, regardless of age, ends in divorce. Lack of finances, unemployment, physical, emotional and mental abuse, and infidelity are usually the main reasons for divorce. Marriage is a very serious commitment, and it shouldn't be taken lightly.

I was married when I was nineteen. My first husband was six years older than me, and I realized later we were incompatible. And to be truthful, I was immature and should have experienced more of life and dated other guys before settling down.

If you have any doubts and have this uneasy feeling something is not right, then wait until you're really sure. Perhaps even a small break from one another with absolutely no contact for three months can be a good idea. If it's real love, then you both will survive and know for sure if it was meant to be.

Not all teenage marriages end in divorce. Several couples I know have stayed married after forty years or more of blissful marriage. Marriages that have lasted the distance of sixty years plus have often been asked, "What are the secrets to a happy marriage?"

So here are the answers and in no particular order:

- reverence
- love
- honesty
- trust
- respect
- commitment
- set good boundaries
- good communication
- compromise
- never gossip about your partner to your family or friends

Choosing a life partner is one of the most important and mature decisions you will ever have to make. I trust that you make your decision on true love for the other person, and if your gut feeling or intuition is telling you, "Don't do it," then trust this. And never get tangled up with a guy who mistreats you, abuses, cheats on you, or controls and manipulates you. Walk away. No, actually start running.

Contraception

In high school, you learn not only in your biology lesson that the sex hormones are working in overdrive but also you will experience this.

There are the boys who want to prove their muscularity and want to make love to anything with a skirt on. Society accepts that boys lose their virginity early, and no one seems to bat an eyelid. Not to be outdone by the boys, some girls seeking popularity will offer their bodies freely to anybody. Sometimes girls lose their virginities by being deceived by a boy confessing true love and saying to the girl, "We love each other, we will eventually get married, so why wait to have sex?" After the act is over the scumbag expresses to his mates the dirty deed is done and moves onto more conquests, with the backlash that the girl is labelled a good lay. Here is an account of one young girl's first sexual experience:

"To realize after the sexual act was over, it wasn't anything like the other girls said or what the library book revealed. He was rough, and the painful penetration of his penis as he broke my hymen and his hard thrusting was all over in a few minutes. He pulled out and ejaculated all his sticky, creamy semen over my belly, leaving me feeling angry and cheated. I always said I wanted to keep my virginity for my husband. Now I feel utterly dirty and ashamed of myself."

Not exactly a beautiful and romantic experience that God intended for the soul purpose of enjoyment and the creation of life.

If you have met someone special, and you both feel that you want to have sex together outside of marriage, then there will be no stopping you. The only way to abstain from sex is to be strong-willed and place God at the centre of your life, read and study the Bible and pray for guidance.

If you have both decided to take your relationship further beyond lip lock or tongue kissing, then the question of contraception should be discussed. Unplanned teenage pregnancies are very high, unwanted babies ending up being aborted or being adopted out to foster homes. Some decide to live together or marry for the sake of the baby or pressure from parents.

There are many contraception devices, the birth control pill, IUD (intrauterine devices), implants, the diaphragm, the rhythm method, condoms, and sterilization. They all are not 100 percent effective, but the most effective one of all is abstinence from the very act of intercourse. Sorry to bring this up, but if you are going to have lots of sexual partners, there's probably a few things that you need to know.

If you have started copulating at an early age and have several partners, chances are this could lead to STD (sexual transmitted diseases) if you aren't careful.

Condoms are highly effective against HIV, gonorrhoea, chlamydia, trichomonas's, and some protection with genital herpes, syphilis, chancroid and HPV. Many sexually transmitted infections have no symptoms at all, but left untreated, those infected can have fertility problems and increased risk of cervical cancer. Those symptoms include genital itching, burning or discomfort, vaginal discharge, swollen lymph glands, rashes, fever or flu-like symptoms or a feeling of pressure in the abdomen. Pain during sex can be caused by possible advanced stage of gonorrhoea and chlamydia infection.

Make sure you carry condoms in your purse so you're not caught out without any protection. As a precaution against pregnancy, insist on your partner wearing a condom during sex, as this will be double protection even if you also use another contraceptive device. Make sure your partner has been checked out with STD blood tests first, especially as he may have had several previous partners. Don't just take his word that he is okay; it's better to be safe before you proceed with the act of sexual intercourse. This may take about five days for test results to come back, so hold off and be strong in saying no.

Check out the copy of the results yourself and do not rely on your partner's word that the test results were negative. If there are positive blood test results, the health department will be notified, and you would have saved yourself a lot of worry.

I know a lot of women and girls are embarrassed and tense up during a pap smear procedure done by their doctor, this causes unnecessary physical pain. The procedure takes less than ten minutes and once you're sexually active, a pap smear is required every two years and is necessary in detecting early cervical cancer. And if your doctor prescribes the birth control pill, then he or she will do a pap smear first.

The most common sexually transmitted infection is human papillomavirus, which there are one hundred types, it is spread by vaginal, anal or oral sex with someone who has the virus. Some types cause genital warts and skin infections, and some types may cause cell changes that lead to cervical cancer, and certain other genital and throat cancers.

The HPV vaccine drug Gardasil is given prior to becoming sexually active, and is protection from two types that cause seventy percent of all cervical cancers. Over the course of twelve months girls aged twelve to thirteen years are given two shots of the vaccination, and is freely supported by the government. You are required to have parental consent, as there are side effects as in any vaccinations.

Please check all the information and together with your parents discuss the pros and cons before you make the decision to be vaccinated against HPV.

Divorce

Approximately 90 percent of all marriages fail, costing the two parties thousands of dollars through the family law court. Not to mention the heartache and stress that it causes to children and the extended family.

You will need to be separated for twelve months before you can apply for a divorce, and using a solicitor is the best procedure.

If there is property involved you and your partner can sell your assets before the divorce proceedings have started.

If there are children involved, the court will be more interested in how each partner can support the child or children. It's a messy business, and all assets including you and your partner's superannuation is included in the assets so definitely have a really good solicitor. Have all your financial business, including child support, finalized through family court before you move into another committed relationship. There are no winners in a divorce. Children are often caught in the middle and left wondering if they are to blame for their parents break up. Children are often used between the parents for retaliation or revengeful attacks. This is pretty low, because children are the innocent ones.

Painful Menstruation

Teenagers often think they are invisible; they have "I can do anything" attitudes. Your hormones are all over the shop, and sometimes painful periods are exasperating at times. For a few certain days of the month, you feel so agitated and emotional that you could kill anything that breathes. You have such a changeable nature all hell breaks loose.

The following suggestions have helped me so I hope you find them useful:

Find a place of calmness out in nature, a place that's comfortable with less stress.

If you have calm thoughts, then internally your hormones will have stability.

The stress hormone cortisol can be elevated thirty times in a day, which can rob your bone health. No need to exercise. Just rest as much as possible during these days.

A relatively new pain relief is a suppository tampon that has been treated (made up of cocaine) and inserted in the virginal cavity, which will bring relief in twenty minutes. Personally I would choose the calm approach, by resting quietly or the use of conventional pain relief is a more sensible approach for painful periods.

An Unwanted Pregnancy

A teenage unwanted pregnancy is possible one of the most stressful, gut-wrenching problems you will have to face. A teenager may feel guilt and shame, because they have to face Mum and Dad, or it's an inconvenience and ruined their plans.

The decision to keep or terminate the pregnancy is among the most agonizing decisions that you will ever encounter. Some even choose to go full term and then adopt their baby out to another couple who are unable to conceive.

I know of a number of young women who have deeply regretted terminating their babies. Some have suffered guilt, shame, and depression as a consequence of their losses. And one unfortunate lady I know has never been able to conceive again when she finally was ready to start a family. There's possibly hundreds in the same situation like her in the world, although there are a number of women who have had one or more abortions and now have become mothers when it was convenient for them. Most girls and their partners see nothing wrong with terminating the foetus, with no thought of their unborn child. Some pregnant teen girls have been forced into marriage because the parents felt their daughters brought shame on the family by being single mums.

Of course, I also know of teenage mums who wanted to keep their babies and were supported by the father and family to keep the baby and have married the father and have added siblings.

Extra-marital Affairs

On another issue of sex outside of marriage, there are plenty of people engaging in extra-marital affairs. Engaging in adultery is a costly mistake that will lead to ruining your reputation and you mistrusting your partner. If you are having sex with a married man and he promises he is going to leave his wife and kids, then you could be waiting a very long time. Even if he does leave his wife and you eventually marry him or live together, every time he is late home, you'll always be paranoid that he is with someone else. It stands to reason that if he cheated on his first partner, he might cheat on you.

On a Personal Note

In no way do I endorse sexual intercourse before marriage. This is entirely up to the parties concerned. It is not God's way either. Read the Bible for it speaks the truth. Abstinence from sex may encourage you to build relationships in other ways. You need to find out what feels right for you and what makes you feel good about yourself. I do not agree with abortion, as I believe that a life has started once an egg and sperm have joined together. Many will disagree, and the only way to form your own opinion is to search your heart and conscience on the matter.

These are God's laws, and you should read the Bible, pray, and search your conscience before making an informed decision. The older generation say morality has slipped into a decline, and they shake their heads in disgust. But it's no different than any other generation when you look back in history. Before, it was hidden, with the master of the manor having his fling with the downstairs maid, and if she became pregnant, he would send her packing in disgrace. I would suggest all young girls read any of the classic Jane Austen's novels. The writer's characters portray life as it was expected to be lived in society in England two hundred years ago.

That is a much different story in the life of a young girl today with so much freedom to make choices.

All God's commandments are for our protection, and strangely enough, we get hurt when we deviate from His ways. Having it all our own way is the sign of the times, and with acceptance of unwanted pregnancies, we have grown further away from God's laws. Babies who were born out of wedlock had the unfortunate stigma of being called "bastards," but thank goodness, that terminology is not really used today in that context. The result is that the contraceptive pill prescribed has given women more freedom to choose when and if they want sex.

It saddens me that in the space of your teenage years that so many grown up issues need to be addressed.

We have covered a lot of moral issues in this chapter, so I hope I have not overloaded you with too much information. These issues are on every girl's mind and lips, becoming like an annoying dripping tap, and you need to pay attention to words of wisdom. Reading God's word, the Bible, talking to your mum or another female adult for their opinions or advice, you will be well informed to make decisions.

CHAPTER 7

DIET, HEALTH, AND FITNESS

Health is the greatest gift, contentment the greatest wealth, faithfulness the best relationship. Buddha

We have all heard the medical professionals tell us we need to be eating healthier and getting more exercise. We have become either a culture of gym fanatics, exercising to the extreme, or couch potatoes, sitting and playing on our mobile phones, using apps or in front of TV and gaming consoles.

Too much of anything can't be good for you. It's all about balance in your life. Your body is a bunch of cells (one thousand trillion), and you have two major fluids, your blood and your lymph. Your blood is pumped around your body and brings in nutrients to the cells and eliminates waste.

Eating poor Nutritional Food is Garbage to your Body
Photo @ Skypixel/Dreamtime.com

Your heart is a muscle that pumps the blood around your body. You need to keep the heart pumping effectively with cardio exercises to keep it strong. It's essential to move your body to work your muscles attached to bones and also to eliminate waste through your lymphatic system.

Think of your lymphatic system as having three kidneys, - one kidney is the skin. The lymphatic system aids the immune system in removing waste, toxins, and pathogens, and it absorbs fats and fat-soluble vitamins from the digestive system. The lymph waste is the thicker fluid, and you need to flush this away, or it will back up like a clogged sewer line. Unlike blood, which flows throughout the body, the lymph flows in only direction, upward toward the neck.

There is no pump for the lymph, so the upward movement depends on the motions of the muscle and joint pumps. As the lymph moves towards the neck, the lymph passes through lymph nodes that filter it to remove debris and pathogens. There are between six hundred and seven hundred lymph nodes in your body, and the role of the nodes is to filter the lymph before it returns to the circulatory system. Lymph nodes can become infected, and you will end up with swollen glands that need to be drained. But it's important to remember lymph nodes are not glands. At the base of the neck, the cleansed lymph flows into the subclavian veins on either side of the neck.

In order to leave the tissues, the lymph must enter the lymphatic system through specialized lymphatic capillaries. Approximately 70 percent of these superficial capillaries are located near the skin. The remaining 30 percent, deep lymphatic capillaries, surround most of the body's organs.

Wear clothing that fits properly, because tight clothing restricts your lymphatic system and contributes to blockage.

Consider alternative therapies

Acupuncture has been found to do wonders for keeping our lymph system flowing.

Regular treatment from a massage therapist who is familiar with lymph drainage massage is a great way to keep your entire body healthy and your lymph system running smoothly.

A simple detox of juicing with a combination of three carrots, three stalks of celery, a half bunch of spinach helps clear your skin, cleanse the kidneys, and cleanse and build blood.

Or consider an apple cider vinegar cleaner.

- 1 cup apple cider vinegar (organic, unfiltered)
- 1 cup raw honey (local is best)
- 8 cloves of garlic

Mix it for one minute on high speed. Put it in a glass container and keep it in the refrigerator for five days. Now, take two teaspoons every morning before breakfast. Be sure to mix it in water or juice. Diluting it makes it very easy to take.

The appearance of cellulite is often a sign of a congested lymph system. Massage the areas of your body where the cellulite exists as well as the lymph nodes in your groin to help improve the condition. You can use sesame oil, almond oil, or coconut oil.

So the answer is simple you need to move and get moving by exercising. Walking briskly at least thirty minutes at least five times per week is recommended.Rebounding on a trampoline for fifteen minutes daily.Dry brushing vigorously on the arms, torso and legs helps eliminate toxins. The brush strokes directions should go from neck and calves to torso.

There are many exercise choices

- tennis, swimming, bike riding, hockeyfast and slow jogging, mix it up, to help burn more fat (twenty minutes slow the ten minutes fast).water or snow skiingcross-country running
- dancing, yoga, tai chi, judobaseball, abseiling
- weight trainingkick-boxing

Just pick a couple you feel comfortable doing, or maybe you would like to learn a new skill. If you haven't exercised in a while, take it slow at first and then gradually build up. It's important to make a habit of exercising daily, and it usually takes twenty -eight days to become a habit.

Make yourself accountable, make a promise to yourself, and write down your commitment on a piece of paper. Stick the paper where you can see it every day- on the bathroom mirror, on the fridge on the bedroom door, in your diary. It doesn't really matter when you exercise, morning or late afternoon, but not before bedtime. Most people choose morning because they are more energized then, rather than later in the day. Now it's easy to make excuses for not exercising, but if you make a promise to yourself and don't break it, you will actually become fitter, well-toned, look and feel great, and be a confident and happier person.

If you can master a daily habit of exercising, you can master anything you set your intentions on.

The benefit of exercising is you will have stronger muscles and bones and will be less prone to injury and fractures now and later on in life. Push your body in a safe way so there will be less injury and do warm-up exercises like stretching beforehand. Also, it's important to do stretches afterwards to loosen tight muscles, as you don't want to be sore after your workout.

Go it alone or join a gym or club. If you don't have the disciple to go alone or just want company, find a buddy and go together. Joining a gym is a fun way to exercise and make new friends. Even if you feel clumsy and uncoordinated, there will be plenty of others in the same situation. But watch out for upfront fees or signing into a contract; it could become expensive if you don't like it. To save money on gym fees, exercise at home by purchasing a skipping rope, a mini-trampoline, a fit ball, a step-up, and some dumb bells, or learn to improvise with whatever you have. Plan to include some walking or swimming daily and you can have an effective workout.

I'm sure most of you who are still at school have a weekly

sports day. I know that when you reach your senior years, you can choose your sports afternoon as a study period and not do sport. Okay, I know what I'm about to say may sound crazy, but it is more beneficial for you to participate in some form of competitive team sport at this time.

When doing my banking in person, I became friendly with the bank teller, as both our sons were doing their higher school certificate in the same year. Her son became dux of his school and applied for the air force to become a pilot. Unfortunately, he wasn't accepted, and one of the reasons, the recruiting officer said, was that he hadn't played any team sport. Playing team sports does have a lot of advantages physically, mentally, and psychologically, and it shows a future employer that you can interact with others as part of a team.

You can study at home later where you will be more refreshed and retain more memory.

Don't confuse playing chess or draughts, which are great for social interacting, with sports. These activities are not going to get your lymphatic system moving. But tai chi and yoga will give you a workout, as they work on exercising all your muscles but at a gentle pace. You could even do these exercises an hour before bedtime.

Drinking plenty of water before, during, and after your workouts will help eliminate the waste products through your liver, kidneys, and skin.

Don't become bored with your workouts, or you will lose motivation and stop altogether, so mix up your routine. If you're exercising to lose weight and reach a plateau, then do something else, like bike riding or skipping. This will help you to stay in shape and give you a chance to recharge your batteries. Once you are motivated again, you will have created a new mind-set and enjoy your workouts again. And the weight will start dropping again. You will be amazed how this works.

Deep Breathing

Deep breathing functions to move our lymphatic fluid around. When we just shallow breathe, we have low energy.

Benefits of deep breathing

- Higher energy
- Our lymphatic fluid moves around and allows our immune system, our white blood cells to do their proper job of removing waste.
- Simply breathing in oxygen helps eliminate pain.
- Great stress release

How to deep breathe

- Breathe in slowly through the nose for 5 seconds.
- Hold your breath for 20 seconds.
- Breathe out for 10 seconds.

Overdoing the Exercising

Yes, it's possible to over exercise and put stress on your body, causing you to cramp up and pull your muscles. Therefore, you need to take exercising slow in the beginning, and don't forget your pre-warm-up stretches and after exercising stretches.

After a couple of hours of strenuous activity, glucose stores are depleted, and when this happens, it brings the nervous system function to almost stop. Marathon runners may reach this point, making continued exertion almost impossible.

Long-distance runners and football players know to eat a high-carbohydrate diet regularly, take glucose drinks during activities that last for forty-five minutes or more, and eat energy rich foods within fifteen minutes after they have finished the activity. During prolonged, high-intensity physical activity, muscles needs for oxygen increases tenfold or more, which increases the production of free radicals in the body. Vitamin E is an antioxidant that defends cell membranes against the oxidative damage of free radicals. Physically active young women who engage in vigorous activities need to make sure they are not deficient in iron. Adolescent female athletes who eat vegetarian diets may be at risk, as iron is an essential component of haemoglobin, the protein that transports oxygen throughout the body.

Menstruation and the high demand of muscle protein myoglobin can cause iron deficiency. Fortified cereals, legumes, nuts, red meats, and green vegetables with vitamin C-rich foods are ideally helpful. Diet, or eating healthy, is very important during your adolescent years, because your body's nutrient requirements have increased to compensate with your body's growing needs and bone development.

The World Health Organization recommends adolescents need high levels of iron and calcium because they are growing rapidly.

With a diet rich in fresh fruit and vegetables for necessary vitamins and minerals and consuming dairy products of milk, yogurt and cheese for calcium which helps with bone health. Protein should be eaten at every meal, about the size of your clenched fist, such food as meat, fish, poultry or legumes or nuts. It's important to eat low carbohydrates for energy and limit high carbohydrates like cakes and biscuits which offer very little nutrition Essential fatty acids consisting avocado, olives, macadamia oil, cold pressed olive oil is better than unsaturated fats like margarine

Try adding extra carrots, oranges, or juicy rock melon to your diet and drinking a green smoothie. Eating more plant food is beneficial for healing and cleansing our bodies, as it helps destroys many pathogenic bacteria, fungus and yeast. Therefore, the more chlorophyll we consume, the better our intestinal flora and overall health will be.

Other healing benefits:

- Helps purify the liver
- Makes body more alkaline
- Increases iron in the blood
- Helps sores heal faster
- Resists bacteria in wounds
- Builds high blood count
- Sunshine raises positive moods in persons with SAD (seasonal affective disorder)
- Cleans and deodorizes bowel tissues
- Counteracts toxins eaten
- Eliminates bad breath

Fuelling Your Body with Living Foods

Fuelling your body with living foods is one way of ruling your body, and I am an advocate of eating healthy foods.

I would be telling you an untruth if I said I always eat healthy, as there have been times where I have swung backwards to unhealthy eating. I've eaten for a period of too much junk or processed food and felt sick and my body ached.

When you're young, you feel you can eat anything, but eventually the chemicals and additives will make you sick and can lead to chronic diseases.

Wise diet planning is to select a variety of foods that deliver nutrients that the body needs. We also need variety, balance, energy (kilojoule) control, and moderation in our meals.

The Five Food Groups

1. Breads, cereals, rice, pasta, noodles
2. Vegetables and legumes
3. Fruit
4. Milk, yogurt and cheese

5.   Meat, eggs, fish, poultry, nuts, and legumes
(Note: Legumes are in two food groups)

To achieve a healthy weight, be physically active, chose a variety of foods from the five food groups, and drink water. Limit foods with saturated fats and added salt and sugar.

Anorexia Nervosa

Today we have a culture where you can never be too thin, and we look to celebrities, models, athletes and other women for inspiration and comparisons.

We are obsessed with looks, and we watch glamorous people with admiration and guidance. From the beginning, family and friends praise us for our weight loss and encourage us to keep going. Telling us how great we look, but no one asks us how we really feel, and we keep losing the weight until we can't stop ourselves.

I was nearly a victim of this terrible disease, anorexia nervosa. I couldn't stop dieting and wanted to get rid of my bulging thighs. I'd drink two diet shakes and juice carrot, celery, or apple on a daily basis. I worked full time, always busy running around, looking after family and doing the home duties. Through gaining knowledge, I learned that doing specific exercises is the only way to tone a body area. I finally woke up to myself after I became sick with a really bad cough that wouldn't go away. I developed a chest infection and agreed to go to the doctors after my parents and friends started to comment how thin I was. Looking back now, I think I thought if I looked thinner in my thighs, then I would be accepted and loved more.

Beware of Eating Disorders
Photo @ Raisa Kanareva /Dreamtime.com

Anorexia nervosa is a mental illness with the highest mortality rate, either dying from medical complications of starvation or from suicide. Patients often refuse treatment, and unfortunately, if not diagnosed early, the illness is harder to treat. Those who are hospitalized are treated by psychiatrists, psychotherapists, medical doctors, and therapists to learn what's behind their emotions and new eating behaviours. Once patients gain weight and are allowed to go home, the danger is they revert back to their old patterns of eating low-fat and low-calorie foods. So they are under strict supervision to gain weight and check-in with their doctors on regular appointments.

B. Timothy Walsh produced a paper in 2013 in which he proposed that for women who are vulnerable to anorexia, weight loss initially serves as a reward, it elicits compliments, relieving anxiety and increasing self-esteem. Overtime, the dieting will be the reward and become habitual. This lack of understanding and lack of treatment is truly an emergency for today's teenagers. They are experiencing a serious mental illness with the highest mortality rate of any psychiatric illness, but our health system, in its current state, is failing them.

Athletes who are top contenders in their sports, will be convinced that they must be specific weight, and will perform better for competition. Participation in sports or competitions, that emphasise a lean appearance, could be severely restricting energy intakes. The prevalence of amenorrhoea among female athletics is high, and no-show periods is characterised by low blood oestrogen, infertility, and often bone mineral losses.

Bulimia

This is an emotional disorder characterized by a distorted body image and an obsessive desire to lose weight. The person will have extreme episodes of overeating and then to compensate by either fasting or self-induced vomiting or purging.

An example would be someone on a yo-yo diet, which is very unhealthy. Hospitalization is vital when you are at your lowest, and the faster the treatment, the quicker the recovery. Unfortunately, once home, your illness can worsen because you're facing reality again, and the emotions you experienced, you're going to face them again.

People who overeat compulsively may struggle with anxiety, depression, and loneliness.

Binge eating is all too common and body weight varies between normal and severe obesity.

For those wanting to help by donations or if you know someone who needs help with any eating disorder, contact: www.thebutterflyfoundation.org.au.

www.nytimes.com/2015/10/13/health/extreme-dieting-of-anorexia-may-be-entreched-habit-study-finds

CHAPTER 8

. . . .

TATTOOS AND BODY PIERCINGS

We only have a few seconds to make a good or bad impression on others we meet for the first time. Our physical appearance, our body language, the words and tone of our speech, our clothes, and our surroundings pretty much say a lot about us.

We can observe others and know that this is a person we would like to hang around with and get to know better. How you express yourself individually will allow opportunities to come into your life or prevent them from doing so.

Before we delve into tattoos and body piercing, another way to create first impressions is in our surroundings. I never realized decluttering is so important in our lives for our health, happiness, and success. This is an area that can make a huge impact on your relationships and financial position. You see, having dust and clutter, stuff you have just laying around, including inside drawers and cupboards that no longer serve you, becomes energy that's stuck. This stuck energy is stale and stagnant and has no vibration as energy should always be moving and is regarded as one of the common causes of poor health according to Feng Shui principles. People often succumb to colds, allergies, and hay fever. Even the air is stale if it's not moving, so open up the windows and doors and let fresh air blow through your bedroom and environment.

A complete clean is essential in your living space, inside and out, several times a year. It is vital that your environment and car are kept clean, free of clutter and anything that needs mending or fixing should be done as soon as possible. You probably are still living at home with your parents, and they do most of the domestic chores in the house and yard. Learn from Mum in the kitchen how she prepares and cooks the food; how she stores the food and separates the cooked food from the fresh food; how she doesn't leave cooked food out on the kitchen bench for hours to breed bacteria. Know the correct way to sort out and wash the clothes, such as delicate underwear or woollen jumpers and-how it's important after you have dried your clothes in the dryer to de-fluff the dryer so it doesn't catch alight, causing a fire from the build-up of lint next time you use it.

DIY All Purpose Cleaner

Mix half cup of vinegar and quarter cup of baking soda into two quarts of water. Adding a little lemon juice or borax will help to make it more potent.

Most homes today have dishwashers, but most kids don't even stack or unstack the dishwasher, always leaving it to someone else. There is no reason or excuse that you can't help and do some chores around the home.

When there are two-income working parents, even taking out the garbage or watering the garden is a huge help. And I'm sure Mum or Dad would really appreciate if you pitched in and shared the chores.

I know it's easy to think you haven't any time to help out with the housework. But ten minutes of picking up your clothes off the bathroom floor or taking the clean clothes off the clothesline would help. And cleaning up the mess from the kitchen cutting board after you used it would be nice for the next person to use.

Sit down, grab a piece of paper, and write down all the things that others do for you. For example, Mum takes me to and from dance class and sometimes drives my friend's home. Dad takes me to netball practice and my Saturday morning game or weekend carnivals. Mum bakes my favourite biscuits and allows my friends to come over for weekend sleep overs. Dad helps me with my homework and school projects when things are difficult. Last Sunday night he drove to the shops in the pouring rain to grab me some paste so I could finish a project that was due the next day.

You get the idea. It's easy to think you are the centre of the universe but realize that a lot of people are running around after you. In return, you can say thank you and that you appreciate what they do for you once in a while.

Making this a habit will always open up opportunities and favours for you now and in the future. Offering to help with the house chores would be really appreciated and shows you are thoughtful. Learning basic skills of becoming a "domestic goddess" will set you up for success when you eventually have a place of your own. As in most things in life, there is an action and a reaction, or two sides to the coin, the positive versus the negative.

Tattoos

- A tattoo was discovered in the mummified preserved skin found on the body of Otzi the Iceman dating between 3370 and 3100 years BC.
- China had tattoos on their mummies 2100-550 BC and used barbaric practices on convicted prisoners faces using symbols, and slaves were marked for ownership.
- Siberian tattooed mummies were discovered, dating around 500 BC, during excavation from burial mounds on the Ukok plateau in the 1990s. The tattoos involved using pictures with animal designs, details of fish, monsters and

a series of dots that linked up along the spinal column and
around the right ankle.

- Egypt used tattoos as a form of healing, religion, and
  punishment.
- Henna is used in body art in India.
- New Zealand Maoris' practiced tattooing known as
  "Tamoko," traditionally created with chisels.
- In Japan between 1603 and 1868 generally firemen, manual
  workers, and prostitutes wore tattoos to communicate their
  status. By the early seventeenth century, criminals were
  visibly marked by crosses, single and double lines, and circles,
  mostly on their faces or arms. These symbols sometimes
  marked where the crime was committed and in one area
  the character "dog" was tattooed on the criminal's forehead.
- In Japan, samurai were regarded as warriors. Under a new
  emperor and new country, the samurai were forced to burn
  their armour. So the warriors adopted a tattoo as a means of
  replacing the armour, but the government banned the practice,
  regarding it as barbaric and lacking respectability. This created
  a problem for the samurai, who were considered outcasts and
  had no place in decent society and were frowned on because of
  their visible tattoos. This forced them into criminal activities,
  which formed the modern-day Japanese mafia.

There are many more examples of tattoos throughout the world,
and the islanders used tattoos for magical qualities and ceremonies.

Samoan society has long been defined by rank and title, with
chiefs and their assistants conducting tattoo markings. These
markings were for the young chiefs during puberty, using sharpened
boars' teeth, fastened together with a portion of turtle shell and a
wooden handle. Part of the ascendance would eventually lead to a
leadership role, but the pain was so extreme.

To back down or to leave the initiation incomplete would be
sign of being a coward and place great shame on the family and

themselves throughout life. The risk of death by infection was possible as the process was five sessions spread over ten days for the inflammation to subside. The dye was made from the soot collected from the burnt lama nuts which they wound grind.

Sir Joseph Banks, a British naval officer who served with Captain Cook on his sea voyages, came back to Britain with a tattoo, as did many seamen.

By the nineteenth century, tattooing had spread to British society but was still largely a tradition and practice with sailors and the lower or even criminal class.

Tattooing was practiced by amateur public school boys by the 1840s, and by the 1870s it became fashionable with the upper class and royalty.

By 1898, one in five members of the gentry were tattooed. British court, George V, Edward VII, King Frederick IX Denmark, King of Romania, Kaiser Wilhelm II, King Alexander of Yugoslavia and Tsar Nicholas II of Russia all had tattoos.

In 1969, the House of Lords debated a bill to ban the tattooing of minors on grounds that it became trendy, to encourage self-identification with criminal groups.

Since the 1970s tattoos have become more socially acceptable and fashionable among celebrities but least prominent on figures of authority.

By 2010, 25 percent of Australians under the age of thirty years had tattoos.

Sometimes woman use tattoos as a marking against a traumatic experience, abuse, or breast cancer (en.wikipedia.org/wkii/History-of-Tattooing).

My father had a couple of tattoos, because he joined the Royal British Navy and later the Royal Australian Navy. Personally I don't have any, but I did consider having a small one and couldn't decide where on my body. Does it hurt? Yes, probably, but that depends on your pain threshold, so I believe. Having worked as a venepuncturist, I've observed plenty of tattoos on the arms of my patients. And I've had many patients say they would rather have a baby or tattoo than a blood test, so go figure.

Many people have very colourful and dainty ones, and some have frightening, satanic tattoos, both with poor and good quality artwork. Consider carefully the design, big or small, and where you want the tattoo inked on your skin. Tattoo ink is generally permanent, and if you change your mind sometime later, a darker cover-up is needed and will be two to five times larger than the existing tattoo.

Tattoo removal is difficult and painful, and the success depends on the materials used. Some claim that it's easy to remove. Others say some ink materials fade with time, leading to a washed-out look. The Food and Drug Administration and medical practitioners have noted that many ink pigments used in tattoos are industrial strength colours like those used in printer' ink or automobile paint.

Tattoo parlours should warn customers that their inks contain heavy metals known to cause cancer, birth defects, and other reproductive harm.

Tattoo Ink Materials

Metal Pigment Base

- Cadmium-red, orange, yellow
- Nickel- black
- Zinc-yellow, white
- Chromium- green
- Mercury- red
- Lead-yellow, green, white
- Cobalt-blue
- Aluminium-green, violet
- Titanium-white
- Iron-brown, red, black
- Barium-white
- Nickel-black

Pigment Bases-Manufactures are not required to reveal their ingredients or conduct trials. Professional inks may be made from iron oxides (rust), metal salts, plastics.

Homemade or traditional may be made from ink, soot, dirt, or blood, which sounds disgusting (en.wikipedia.org/wiki/tattooing).

A recent case report also showed that tattoo pigments migrate into lymph nodes, which is scary.

Besides infection from unsterile needles, exposure with heavy metals is a risk of allergic reactions, eczema and scarring. Medical MRIs can cause tattoos to burn or sting, as the ink is affected by the tests magnetism.

Carrier

Carriers act as a solvent to carry the pigment from the point of needle to the dermis of the skin. Carriers keep the ink evenly mixed and free from pathogens and aids in the application. Ethyl alcohol, water, denatured alcohol, methanol, propylene glycol, and glycerine are also used.

Don't be afraid to check out the reputation of the tattoo parlour, look for referrals, check out its website, and ask other customers. Find out the quality and designs of the tattooist and the materials or pigments they use beforehand. You may want a particular design, so firstly, find out if your tattooist can do the work and then get a quote.

Perhaps another tattooist who works there on another day is more qualified to do your particular design. Don't be pressured into accepting a design that you're not totally happy with. It takes a lot of hours and work by the tattooist to come up with an agreeable piece of artwork.

You will need to pay a deposit, and this money is non-refundable if you can't turn up for your appointment and give less than two days' notice. You will forfeit the deposit if you don't make another new appointment. And most places are unable to accept cancellations over social media or by email, as they are way too busy to keep checking these devices. So make sure you follow and check the small print before signing over your hard-earned cash or credit card.

Warning

You must make sure the facility is reputable and sterile, the autoclave is working correctly, and the operator knows how to use the equipment correctly. Dirty needles and unsterile equipment are causes of great concern, and hepatitis B, C, tuberculosis, mycobacterium, syphilis, malaria, and HIV is possible

(Scientificamerican.com/article/tattoo-ink).

Tattoo manufactures consider their ingredients list proprietary information, but some brands do release information.

Now for the good news: it's possible to have non-toxic tattoo ink ingredients.If you are concerned about toxic ink, then the least toxic ink is black.

Black Ink is the Least Toxic Ink
Photo @ Frank and Danielle Kaufmann/Dreamtime.com

Avoiding brightly coloured or neon pigments, which may require the use plastics and natural ingredients. Red pigments often cause allergic reactions in both toxic and non-toxic, so avoid this colour altogether is my advice.

If your heart is set on red, there are some brands that make an extra effort to ensure safe non-toxic inks such as Eternal, Skin Candy, Dynamic and Kuro Sumi.

After Care

- Don't re-bandage unless advised.
- Don't pick or scratch your tattoo.
- Avoid hot tubs and swimming while healing.
- Avoid direct sunlight and tanning beds.
- When you get home, dispose of your bandage and wash your tattoo thoroughly with a mild antimicrobial soap and warm water.
- Apply and rub completely a thin layer of ointment into the skin and re-apply twice a day for two weeks.

Minimum price for a tattoo varies. You'll pay for quality, but a small one costs around $50-$110. Larger work of five hours or more, including multiple sessions, are priced at an hourly rate, usually $200 per hour. So always get a quote and know precisely if cash only is paid for each session on the day.

Some businesses don't have credit card facilities. And you will need to be 18 years of age.

Body Piercing

Ears

I think that for most people, having your ear lobes pierced and adorning the ears with beautiful jewellery is acceptable. But when it comes to other parts of the body, such as oral, facial, torso, or genital, then society tends to frown upon this.

The **ear lobe** is the most common, as it's quick, easy, low pain, and healing takes about six to eight weeks.There are other parts of the ear that are pierced, such as conch and helix (inside and outside of ear), rook, and daith.

Facial piercings involve the septum of the nose, nostril, and bridge of nose, eyebrow and "nasaling." Nasaling is quite rare and looks scary, because the piercing passes through one nostril, through the inner cartilage of the nose, and back through the other nostril.

Oral

Lips are common, easy, and heal quickly, but you will have swelling, so you will require downsizing of initial jewellery. This is often done in pairs for a unique look.

Tongue is easy and fast healing, but expect to talk funny. Downsizing is required once swelling has gone down. Eating can be uncomfortable during the first week. Pain is low and healing time is four to twelve weeks.

Webbing is under the tongue or inside the top lip or inside the bottom lip.

Cheeks are more difficult to heal as they pass through a very mobile muscle in your face. It's usually done by a thicker gauge needle to obtain faster healing and increased comfort.

Industrial Piercing these are also known as scaffolds and are visible and decorative but are just two cartilage piercings linked together. They are the funniest piercings to do, but you need to be careful during healing not knock the piercing, as they are can cause scar tissue and prolong healing. Pain level is medium and healing time is eight to sixteen weeks.

Dermal anchors go virtually anywhere, and they have an L-shaped base with a head at the top and are quite small. They are held inside the body through tissue growing in between small holes. Rejection is a concern, and they can be easily changed in the studio.

Corsetry piercings are in different positions, and then you can thread ribbon through each hole in a crisscross effect, and this looks like a corset.

Nipple Piercings cannot be done under the age of eighteen, even with parental consent. Ring can be worn, or a straight bar is better for healing. Takes six to eighteen weeks to heal.

Genital Piercings require that you be eighteen years-plus, but these are more common than you think. The wearer experiences increased stimulation as well as being aesthetically pleasing, so the leaflet says. Yeah, right. Shaving is recommended before, and protected sexual activity can resume once you feel comfortable- ouch! Generally, wait four to six weeks. Pain level is said to be low to high, but I'd give this definitely a high. Healing takes four weeks to four months.

Female- outer and inner labia, Christina, Isabella, princess Albertina, clitoral etc.

Healing

- Inflammation (one week) - swelling, redness, bleeding - ice
- Yellow crusters (two to four weeks) - don't pick them
- Matured (five weeks) - red gone, keep cleaning
- Downsize (six weeks) - change to smaller jewellery

After-care Advice

- Don't sleep on or pump your piercings.
- Oral piercings that are constantly played with may rip and cause scar tissue.
- Don't use alcohol wipes, Dettol, Betadine, Listerine or any harsh products will harm your piercings.
- Saline rinses and Aspro-Clear can help to eliminate crusters.
- Low carat gold or sterling silver is not advisable to wear three to six months.

For body piercing and tattooing, you need to be eighteen years old unless accompanied by a legal guardian. Both need photo ID, guardian or parent needs a Medicare card with both names on it or paperwork verifying their legal guardianship.

I have been in the health industry for quite a number of years, and my work as a venepuncturist for twenty-four years I have seen many patient's tattoos.

Personally, I don't like a lot of body piercings or tattoos I've seen, and it's not that I am a prude, maybe a wimp, though. But I will always remember this lovely elderly lady who I became acquainted with, as she came to give blood on a regular basis.

She had been coming for a while, and out of the blue, she said, "I'm really embarrassed and ashamed of my tattoo."

I asked her, "Why?" And she told me the story of when she was in her thirties and became a born-again Christian. She had been asked by the pastor of her church to go meet a troubled run away teenage girl at the central train station in Sydney.

My patient met the teenage girl and took her to a safe house, and it was some years later that they met again, and the now young woman told her rescuer. "The only reason I went with you is I knew you had been one of us, because you had a tattoo."

There is always a reason for something. God used my elderly patient to allow this young teenager, who incidentally married a pastor, and now has a family of her own, to feel comfortable. If you have tattoos that you are now regretting, well, just think about that story. It could just as well have been a different story for this run away adolescent.

Think carefully about what tattoo or tattoos you're placing on your body, the design, the ink colours, or your body piercings. Remember: first impressions count. If they are uncovered, it says a lot about you before you even open your mouth.

I showed pictures of two teenagers to ten different business owners, from corporate, manufacturing, and retail companies and asked if they would give them a job.

The first one had facial body piercings, a lip ring, eyebrow ring, small diamond nose stud, and outer ear studs, starting from the lobe finishing at the top and a tongue stud. She also had a small, coloured snake tattoo twisting around her neck and writings of names or quotes on both wrists.

The second woman had a couple of earlobe piercings in each ear, and you could see a tiny butterfly on her ankle. Both women were then asked to come in for an interview and had equal educational qualifications with bubbly personalities and you could see they had similar looks. Now who would be the first choice for the job?

Well, that's hard to say. It would depend if the job was corporate, manufacturing, or retail. Now, even though I said they had similar looks, I didn't say what they were wearing. If the women with the most body piercings and tattoos was wearing a classic, stylish pant suit and was applying for a corporate or retail job, would she have a better chance in the interview? Or the woman with the least body piercings and tattoos, if she wore a neat casual pair of genes and top? And that's why first impressions make a huge difference to others, and if you can prove that you were unfairly treated by an employer, then you should speak up. Sometimes life isn't fair, but making things appear invisible using makeup coverage has its advantages.

If they were both applying for the manufacturing job, then who do you think would likely get the position? Just on observation: maybe the second women with the least body piercing as the jewellery might become a machinery hazard.

But then what if the first woman was asked to not wear all the jewellery? Perhaps she would be offended and not willing to do that, and she would have a reason that she was discriminated against.

What first impressions are you sending out to others? It may be the difference between getting the job or not and how people treat you?

CHAPTER 9

· · · · · * * * ● * * * * · · ·

SQUARE PEG IN A ROUND HOLE

Ever try to put a square peg in a round hole? It doesn't fit, does it no matter how many times you try? It's the same with people. We aren't the same. Some are round, and others are square. Some people are workaholics, other are lazy, and some are underachievers. Or they may feel superior and think they are better than others. Others are selfish, conceited, and bad mannered, while others are helpful and considerate.

If you have a negative attitude and a bitter heart and you spray hurtful words to others, this is what you will receive back. This is called the law of attraction: whatever you sow is what you will reap. If you have love in your heart for others, then you will spray goodness over everyone and everything. "Do unto others as they would do unto you."

Racism should not be tolerated, and it is an offence to belittle others because of a difference of opinion. It is important to interact with others with respect to their customs, beliefs, language, and history. One should be treated equal, regardless of race, physical appearance, religion, sexual preference, age, and education. Australia is a multicultural country, and people have come from all over the world to make this country their home.

Name calling in the early days and up until the twentieth century was mostly just in jest and fun until someone just got riled up and took offence. I think there will be indifference. Look how the British tried to wipe out the true custodians of Australia, calling them "savages" and segregating them onto small sections of land. The British took over the land and made it their own to grow their own food crops and build towns, sending the Aborigines further into the scrub. And they brought diseases and nearly wiped out the indigenous communities.

Because indigenous Australians roamed this land freely for thousands of years, they had their own laws and knew the ways of the seasons and stories of dream time. No one has the right to take away the land and customs from the original land owners. Isn't that how disagreements and segregation starts, with greed and taking over the ownership of the land with its abundance of resources?

Hopefully, with a lot of common sense, there will a treaty, and I pray that we can all live together in harmony. It starts with you and me tolerating our differences and believing that we are all equal regardless of our colours, education, sex, customs, and religions.

Bullying

There's many types of bullying, both direct and indirect.

Direct bulling is hitting, kicking, punching, name-calling, and insulting. Indirect is the subtle type of non- physical bullying that isn't easily viewed by others, your boss, other workers and students, or teachers. It can be rude hand gestures, pulling faces, turning backs, and threatening or weird looks. Spreading rumours, gossiping, blackmailing, breaking secrets, criticizing clothes or personalities, whispering, excluding you, and even stealing friends are other forms of indirect bullying. Damaging another person's social reputation, peer relationship and someone's self-esteem is all classified as bullying.

On line bullying, or cyber bulling, is sending abusive texts or emails to others to cause physiological harm. Taking photos of others that are unflattering to them or naked ones and sharing on social media sites is bullying. It's hard to escape nasty comments that are posted on social media, as it can go viral within hours. If you can't ignore the comments, then let your parents or an adult know what's going on. As this is a criminal offence and you know the person, then report it to the police. Let the authorities do their jobs and handle it. Switch off all the social media sites, even your mobile phone, and talk to someone about how you're feeling. Don't bottle all your emotions inside. It's natural to be afraid, angry, and depressed, but it's going to be alright. There is professional help.

Call Lifeline or the sites especially for teens, such as Beyond Blue or Head Space. Phone numbers are at the end of this chapter. Call your school counsellor and let him or her know what's going on. You may need to take some time away from school or work for a few days. Never be afraid or worry how people will react to your situation. They aren't wearing your shoes.

Help is always within reach. God is a good listener and ready to send in his army to fight your battles for you. If you know of someone who is being bullied and you are an observer and you do nothing, then you are just as guilty as the abuser. The right thing to do is to intervene and offer assistance and comfort to the one being bullied.

Unfortunately, often no one wants to get involved, so they turn blind eyes to the attack in case the abuser turns on them and they become victims themselves. A bully thinks it's fun to pick on someone who he or she knows is afraid and intimidated by them. The bully is the tough, strong one, usually a controller who thinks it makes them popular.

Why do they do it?

Perhaps for leadership amongst their peers, lack of knowledge, jealousy, misunderstanding, distrust, fear, or they were once victims themselves. You know the saying: "Children learn from adults."

It could be the parents are bullies also. They see aggression as acceptable, and there is no concern about the rights of others.

I express gratitude for those who have chastised, condescended, and ridiculed me. I am appreciative of those who were spiteful, cruel, and vindictive. I thank them for their manipulation, disdain, anger, jealousy, and resentment. For through these experiences, I have learned so much about how not to behave. I have been the victim of bullying on two occasions, both with verbal attacks in front of several others who witnessed the whole incident.

How did I handle the situation?

I just froze, completely embarrassed and then angry, and I didn't say a word, although I thought of several words I could have said at the time afterwards.

Did anyone stick up for me and say anything or agree with the bully? Nothing was said on both occasions, and in both instances, the bully was misinformed with information that wasn't correct. The matter dropped, and the bully strutted her stuff, ready to attack the next victim for a fight.

In a situation where the bully does repeat the bullying, then more action is required. When you are unprepared and ridiculed by somebody's stinging remarks, it does put you off guard. But I have vowed to myself that I will never let myself be in this situation again. It's funny how life throws you the same lessons to learn over and over until you get a pass. Hopefully, you'll get a distinction mark the next exam. Being passive and being aggressive are both unbalanced, but being assertive is appropriate. I've thought about what I could have said, so here are some ideas you can say that will bamboozle the bully.

- "Thank you for sharing your comments. That's called freedom of speech."
- "Would you repeat what you said but more slowly?"

- "Are you trying to make me feel bad about myself, because I'll just pass those comments on?"
- "That's not going to work, because I'm not accepting what you said about me."

If this doesn't help, well, instead of retaliating, walk away and live another day, as the saying goes. It could become a physical contact, so never throw the first punch, bite, or hair pull, and I hope you can defend yourself. A bully knows how to fight, sometimes dirty, though. She won't want to lose and come away second best.

So what if you are the bully? Well, I'll probably say that you are good leadership qualities; you're not afraid to speak your mind and you are assertive and have high self-esteem and good verbal skills and could talk yourself out of trouble.

These a pretty good traits and all positive attributes, so what's not to like about you? But wouldn't it be better to stop the bullying altogether? You would be popular with all your peers and teachers.

But what about if you are a bully who has a low opinion of yourself? You're not the ideal weight. Let's say you're hugely over weight, so you become depressed and so very angry that for protection, you lash out at everyone you come in contact with. You become the bully for your own self-preservation, so you won't be picked on and become a point of ridicule and nasty comments. You eventually actually liked being overweight, as it gave you power and strength to push people around and into being afraid of you. Then I would say you have poor anger management skills, and you use your huge weight as a crutch to hide from people.Of course, you don't like school and don't like people and hate all the teachers.

Can you not see the difference between the good and bad evil of the bully? The bully can turn her positive attributes into empowerment for herself and, with a kind nature, become the leader in anything she chooses.You will enjoy life more because life with give you more opportunities to fulfil your dreams and goals. Don't waste your talents- use them for a purpose of good for yourself and others. The bully with the low opinion of herself, well, unless she gets help from a counsellor, she will always play the blame game even as she is older. She will have a miserable existence and possibly disassociate from others who finally wakeup to her moans about how hard done by she is.

Sexuality

Same sex couples (homosexuality), opposite sex (heterosexuals) couples, either (bisexual), changed their birth sexual organs (transgender), we all have a preference.

History tells us homosexuality has been around since Greek and Roman times. Punishment for same- sex couples has been imprisonment, drowning, or being cast down with rocks.But homo sapiens is the only species in nature that is thought to hate homosexuality.

Homophobia is someone who has an intense fear or hates homosexuals. Men are called fags, gays, or shirt lifters, and women are called lesbians or dykes.

To most homosexuals, what is termed as "coming out," where they actually tell their family and friends they are gay, is how different people treat them. For the majority of people, including family, it is shock, disgusting, and shameful, and it is still taboo in some circles.

I know personally two families whose sons are homosexual. One son was an only child, and while it was a shock to the parents, he was accepted and their relationship remained the same. The other was the youngest son in the family and the parents were appalled and would have nothing to do with their son.

The hardest rejection is from fathers not excepting their sons are gay, and that's why many choose not to tell. Some work away and live overseas for fear of their families finding out.

I'm not sure, but I'm assuming that for lesbian women there is less fuss being made as it's more acceptable. Most of the time that girls and boys aren't even sure who they prefer, some are bisexual.

You may be disgusted with someone's sexually, and you may not like it, but we aren't all the same. Some are round, and others are square, remember? But all deserve and want to be loved. Those who jump up and down the most are usually the one's watching the annual Mardi Gras on television. So how can you tell if a girl is a lesbian, as she doesn't have a tag placed upon her clothes, or she's not impregnated with a chip under her skin?

There is some tell-tale signs, but be cautious: she may not be a dyke; the only way of telling is to ask directly. They are usually the life of the party, always moving as they talk, with expressive facial and artistic mannerisms. They speak with such flair and excitement that you wonder if they should become actresses. Their appearances can be different. Some dress flamboyantly and have great fashion sense. Others dress in tomboy styles with baggy or low-slung pants, or suits with short jackets.

Why do I scream at everyone and bang doors or throw things and then start crying?

Angry Girl Screaming
Photo @ Maksym Bondarchuk/Dreamtime.com

Adolescence is a difficult time when your body's hormones are rapidly changing and you are trying to find independence. It feels like you're sitting on one side of the fence, clinging to childhood, and on the other side womanhood is looming in the future, and it's scary because it's unknown. Your mind rebels against all authority, adults, parents, and teachers, and you fight back by raising your voice, slamming doors, and throwing objects.

Your friends even bug you some days. You constantly argue and scream bad language back and forth at each other, and the next day you have kissed and made up. Parents usually are at the receiving end of your verbal attacks when you don't get your own way. Words spoken in retaliation are hurtful.

Believe it or not, your parents have walked your road already. They do know what you are going through. They love you unconditionally and set rules for your benefit so you don't make the same mistakes they, or others may have. You will realize in many years later that it was your parents or those caring for you, who were protecting you from harm or making huge mistakes.

My Own Journey

Sharing painful experiences with others is one way for you to understand that you are not alone in your own insecurities and challenges.

Personal development is an area that can soar you into places that will inspire you to do amazing things that you never thought you could accomplish. And it can also pull you down into far deepening experiences and emotions that will show you your fears and negative traits. But you will be inspired too as you learn that this is necessary as you go into your inner space and bring out your demons.

I was a very shy, quietly spoken child, the youngest in the family, with two elder brothers. An average child at school, my report cards always said the same thing: "Quiet girl and really tries." And I never got into trouble. I always had friends, but I was not classed as one of the popular girls, though I always had a best friend.

When I was about twelve years old, I was very tall and skinny for my age. To make matters worse, I wore single-wired top and bottom braces to straighten my teeth, which I had to remove from my mouth every time I wanted to eat food. I remember having to visit my dentist weekly and then monthly over a period of a couple of years. Each time the dentist would tighten my braces up as my teeth were relining back into what should be their normal position, and it was a painful experience. There was this one time when my class teacher asked me to read a paragraph out of a book, after my visit to the dentist the day before. My words came out stuttering and splattering, and I stopped and started, and I just wanted to crawl into a big hole. I was so relieved when he finally said I could sit down.

This was totally humiliating, frustrating, and embarrassing, with my self-esteem and confidence extremely shattered just when I was reaching puberty. I tell you the story because if you have ever been humiliated, embarrassed, and frustrated, I can also relate to your pain. Once you identify your painful emotions, write them down on a sheet of paper and, along each one, write how each one has affected you.

Then close your eyes and picture the same scene perfectly before the class teacher and students. This will enforce that, the next time you are asked to do something in a similar situation, you will view it in a positive light. You can even do this for presentations, speeches, and job interviews, or even before going on dates with boys. I guess for most of my growing up years I was a people pleaser, and yes, I still need to check in with myself. Whenever I'm asked to do something and I really don't want to, I now say, "I'll get back to you and let you know in a couple of days." That way I can think more carefully about the idea or suggestion and be more informed.

When you are always saying yes to everybody, even though you don't want to do it, then you are essentially going to burn yourself out, which is not good for your health. You're not loving yourself, because you're choosing them over yourself, and you come out second best. And by not placing yourself first you're telling others that they can walk all over you. Look, you don't have to be selfish, but you can't always be a yes person all your life either.

Take it from me: the sooner you start to take the oars and be the captain of your own boat, the sooner you will feel more empowered and conquer new horizons.

I'm writing this so that you know I'm a real person and not someone who doesn't feel your pain. I know my well- meaning parents loved me, but being such a gentle, sensitive person, I felt alone sometimes, as if I never fitted in. I'm sure they never thought anything was wrong in my life, because I never told them how I really felt.

Did you ever feel the same, and can you relate to what I've just said? Then please, you have a voice, so use it and be your authentic self. Tell them how you really feel, what's going on in your life. Maybe you would rather be doing something else instead. Sure, they may be hurt and upset, but you know they will get over it.

> Be who you are and say what you feel, because those
> who mind don't matter and those who matter don't
> mind - Unknown

Confidence

In my opinion there is nothing more important than your own self-belief in your potential for success and happiness, regardless of your age, gender, looks, education, religion or background. Self-confidence isn't something you were born with, because it's something you develop as you go through life.

When you were a baby, nobody told you, that you couldn't walk. In fact, your parents and everybody encouraged you to take those first steps. You fell down, hurting yourself many times, but you just kept pulling yourself back up until you could eventually walk.

What happened as you became older? You still were determined to do things, but now you were constantly reminded of your faults and shortcomings from others, more than your abilities and successes. Now you need to rewire your brain and opinion about yourself and recognize that you are a unique person. No one else has exactly your temperament, history, experiences, fingerprints, footprints, genetic code, talents, capabilities, and skills. Nobody else is responsible for your life but you, so why give the power to someone else?

Just accept yourself for what you are, because if you can't, certainly no one else will. Break the limiting belief that you aren't good enough. Don't numb yourself to trials and difficulties, nor try and escape your problems, but confront them head on. This will give you more confidence, happiness, and self-worth. This, in turn, will lead you to make decisions and act on them better.

Comparing yourself to others can be positive because it will help you improve yourself. But insisting that you must be good or perfect at everything will only make you anxious, depressed, ineffective, and negative. This misery will lead to procrastination, withdrawal, and even quitting.

Girlhood is a time of identity formation, self-discovery, friendship, and growth. The book of Proverbs in the Bible, addressed specifically to young people, is essentially a book about pure living and wise decision-making. And as this book advises, just be your authentic self, don't be a people pleaser, say what you mean without being unkind, do what you say, and you will be looked upon as a person with integrity.

CHAPTER 10

· · · · · · · · · ● · ● · · · · · · · · ·

THE POWDER ROOM

Hair Removal

Attitudes towards body hair vary between different cultures and individuals. In most Mediterranean countries, it is considered normal for a woman to have hair growth above the upper lip. When I first started working as a venepuncturist some twenty-five years ago, part of my duties was to go to different patients in their homes and collect their blood for testing, ordered by their doctor. During one of my home visits I walked into the bedroom, and my patient was sitting up in bed with this dark-haired, full-growth moustache. Wow. It was even better than my husband's, and the patient definitely wasn't concerned -it was all normal.

This just confirms that we aren't the same if you live in Australia. Being multicultural, we have different views on everything. Even the growth of underarm hair is considered sexy by men. For the majority of Caucasian females, we like smooth, clear skin and dislike it when some bodily hair is showing. During the summer months is generally the busiest time for beauty therapists as their clients will de-fuss their eyebrows, upper lip, thighs, back and front legs, underarms and bikini line. The Brazilian involves total hair removal from the pubic area; it's painful and high maintenance. The Californian, also known as the "Mohican," is not quite total, and a small line of pubic hair is left centrally in a vertical line, which allows a narrow-cut thong bikini to be worn.

There are various types of hair removal, and your choices will be governed by value for money, painless, fast and easy, safety risks and side effects. You can do your treatment at home or at a salon, such as waxing, shaving, plucking, sugaring treatments, threading, pre-waxed strips, abrasives, and depilatory creams.

Each hair grows from a narrow, tube-like depression in the skin called a hair follicle. The base of the hair follicle surrounds the dermal papilla. This area has an abundant supply of blood vessels that bring nourishment to the hair. Hairs are soft at the base but gradually harden and die as they approach the surface. Hair stops growing when it's removed from the source of nourishment.

Laser Hair Removal

Hair removal has become big business with laser hair removal gaining popularity over the last fourteen years. It is relatively new so nobody knows the real side effects to this treatment.

How does laser work? Laser removal works by directing concentrated light into the hair follicle to stop the hair from growing without damaging the skin's surface. Recommended treatments are four to ten treatments spaced six weeks apart. Laser hair removal doesn't work on greying hair, only pigment hair, and you will need to inform the therapist if have been recently sunburnt or tanned, if you're taking medication, or if you have a fake tan. Results are never guaranteed, but you can expect an 80 percent reduction in hair removal. I, unfortunately, didn't have a good result as not all my hairs on my upper lip were dark.

You will need to stay out of the sun, as a tan increases the risk of skin lightening. Wait until tan fades completely, up to six weeks. Shaving is okay, but avoid plucking, waxing, and electrolysis, as these hair removal methods can disturb the hair follicle and interfere with laser hair removal.

After treatment, you will need to avoid hot showers, baths, spas, or saunas for a day or two and extreme sun exposure for two to four weeks regardless of your skin type. Additional maintenance treatments every six to twelve months is advised. Almost all of the body is safe for laser hair removal except around the eye area, which isn't recommended, and you should be given goggles to wear during the treatment. Check if you need any preparation, as some salons say to shave three days before your treatment.

Does it hurt? Well that depends on your pain threshold, it felt like a rubber band popping against my skin. Not every zap will hurt as some areas hurt more such as the lower legs than the thighs so I have been told. You could take a pain relief capsule or I have also heard people applying numbing cream to the skin an hour before the treatment. I don't know if the cream will affect the success of the treatment, so check with the salon first.

How safe is laser removal? Unfortunately, the industry isn't regulated, so you need to be careful where you choose to get your hair removal done. Because it's new, the industry doesn't know if there are any long-term side effects, such as cancer or other complication for the patient.

You need to be cautious about spas, salons and nonmedical personnel who do laser hair removal. Treatment certified by a doctor or registered nurse in dermatology or the cosmetic industry with experience is the better option.

Those who perform the treatment are at risk, as there are potentially harmful toxins such as benzene, toluene, ethyl benzene, diethyl phthalate, and many more. This foul-smelling black smoke plume can release during the procedure and trigger asthma and irritate the airways. Machines should have smoke evacuators and better filtration masks. As a patient or client, you have the right to ask what health and safety standards are in place.

Laser hair removal doesn't guarantee permanent hair loss, as some hairs are resistant or grow again, but the new hair will be finer or lighter. A risk of pigment changes is possible as the affected skin may darken of lighten, although this is temporary. Skin lightening can affect those with dark skins, especially if an incorrect laser is used at an incorrect setting.

It's rare to get blistering, crusting, scarring, and other changes in skin texture. A minimal side effect is redness, but this should disappear in two days. Applying a cooling gel will help to reduce redness and inflammation and also kills bacteria.

Burns can be mild or severe and occurs if the skin absorbs the laser beam and not the hair follicle. Another uncommon problem can occur include greying of treated hair or paradoxically hair might grow excessively in or around treated areas. Most technicians or staff are not properly trained and is a concern, so use discretion for your safety (http://www.mayoclinic.org/tests-procedures/laser-hair-removal/basics/how-you-prepare/PRC-20019438).

Deep Tissue Massage

The magic of hand massage on your body promotes healing through a pain-to-pleasures experience. Deep tissue work breaks up organisms and debris and breaks up the bad calcium deposits in the system and on the bones.

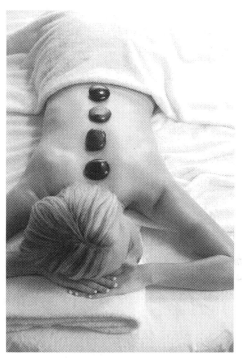

Hot Stone Massage
Photo @Photoroller/Dreamtime.com

Because removing the toxins allows the immune system to work efficiently. I use an essential oil blend of jojoba oil and safflower oil with vitamin E and vitamin F, which helps to provide deep skin-conditioning and calming effects. Massage has many proven detoxifying benefits that include increasing and improving microcirculation and enhancing lymphatic drainage. Most of the immune systems activity occurs in the area surrounding the mouth and front of the neck. There are about thirty lymph nodes in the neck area and any block in this area can have a long-time effect on the body. When you have stress and tension in your life and you feel a tightness in the neck area, maybe it's time for a massage.

This is something you can do yourself and easy to do after you have had your shower or bath.

Sunshine

Being a sun lover, I exposed myself to the sun's rays and would tan easily to a glorious, golden tan. Every summer I would head down to the beaches on the South Coast of eastern Australia and bask in the great outdoors. We all know the dangers of too much sun exposure and how it can prematurely age us and damage the DNA of our cells. If I know I will be going outdoors, I will apply SPF 15 sunscreen lotion twenty minutes before sun exposure and re-apply throughout the day.

Wearing a wide brim hat and UV sunglasses for protection of our eyes and face is also wise.

The exception is that I will expose my body without sunscreen for fifteen minutes daily after 4.00 p.m. and enjoy the summer sun. And during winter twenty-five minutes of sun exposure daily is recommended, as we need the sun's rays so our body can convert this to vitamin D for strengthening our bones and supporting our immune systems. It's uncanny that most Australians are vitamin D deficient.

History

Castor oil was used in ancient Egypt as a protective balm. Skin creams made of beeswax, olive oil, and rosewater were used by the Romans. In ancient Greece and Roman times, women would sometimes make sure their skins were pale by painting their faces with lead paints and chalk. A few centuries later, women even used arsenic (a strong poison) to have pale skin. Pale faces were a trend during the sixteenth century, and women would often bleed themselves to achieve pale skin. The Chinese stained their fingernails with gum Arabic, gelatine, beeswax, and egg white around 3000 BC. Colours for the royal class were gold and silver, and later royals used red and black. The lower class were forbidden to wear bright colours. In Japan, geisha women wore lipstick made from crushed safflower petals. During the Middle Ages in Europe, church leaders thought it was sinful to wear makeup.

In medieval and Elizabethan times, the only persons who had tans were those from the working class, because they worked outside. The upper classes had pale skin, indicating they did not have to labour in the fields. Even the lower class would use white powder to make themselves look like they belonged to the upper class. When transport became more available and people started travelling to holiday destinations by the sea, a change in attitudes began to take place.The wealthy people then spent time in the sun (getting a tan), and this changed the way society viewed tans

(http://www.cosmeticsinfo.org/Ancient-history-cosmetics).

Australian people love their outdoor activities, but it has come with a price, with Australia recording the highest rate of skin cancer in the world. That sun-kissed glow looks healthy and attractive, but you need to be sensible. Evan tanning beds are dangerous and are banned. Prolonged sun exposure, particularly during the hottest times of the day, should be avoided. The skin is especially susceptible to free-radical damage from sunlight.

The sun is one of the most potent natural carcinogens, so ultimately we must protect our skins from excessive sun exposure to prevent photoaging and the potentially damaging effects of skin cancer. Application of sun protection creams and lotions need to be applied several times a day when outdoors, even when it is cloudy.

How safe are our sunscreens? Well, you only have to read the long list ingredients on the bottle or tube to find out. That's if you can pronounce the names. They don't appear that safe to me with all those ingredients, which means it's not natural at all. There are products and services in the beauty industry that can actually cause more long-term harm than good, so know your ingredients. Sunblock products contain one or more of the following harmful additives, oxybenzone, avobenzone, octisalate, octocrylene, homosalath, and octinoxate, and you will be at risk. Oxybenzone is the most common ingredient used and manufacturers use a retinyl palmitate, a form of Vitamin A that increases your risk of skin cancer when exposed to the sun's UV rays (http://www.org/2015sunscreen/report/the problem-with-vitamin-a/).

You also need to choose a sun block that doesn't contain the commonly used synthesized zinc oxide and titanium dioxide. These active ingredients are manufactured in nanoparticle form, naturally small, which is harmful and easily absorbed into the skin. You can purchase all-natural or organic sunscreen of non-lotions online and in the retail shops but nanoparticle versions (zinc oxide is preferred). Not only do berries (especially strawberries) taste great, but they are also great for your skin and offer some UV protection. This antioxidant-rich food will boost your skin's complexion while helping to fight off those damaging free-radicals. A glass of hot green tea can help to fight sun damage and leave your skin hydrated and fresh. Astaxanthin (a potent carotenoid) found naturally in salmon, the pigment that colours the fish pink, can be bought as a supplement offers some protection from the sun. Also, shea butter offers protection also from the sun's rays. Some common sense is required so cover up as much as possible in the middle of the day, wear a wide brim hat and wear good sun UV protection sunglasses.

Feminine Hygiene

Tampons and pads both contain chlorine (a bleaching agent), dioxins, plastics, synthetic fibres and petrochemical additives, synthetic fragrances, and chemical based odour neutralize.Dr. Joseph Mercola, "Women Beware: Most Feminine Hygiene Products Contain Toxic Ingredient"http://www.huffintonpost.com/dr-mercola/feminine-products b 3359581.html.).

Because these products are classified under medical devices, manufactures can add ingredients without disclosure of what they are.

Tampons-bleached, toxic by-products, dioxins and furans that can cause harm of the reproductive organs, endocrine disruption and cancer.

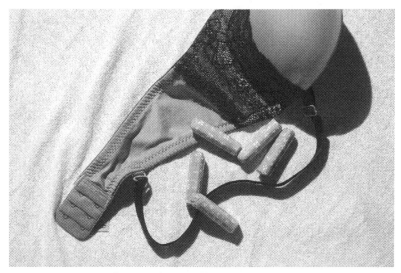

Awareness of toxic chemicals in our Feminine Products
Photo @Colicaranica/Dreamtime.com

Pads-all of the same risks as bleached tampons with added risk of adhesive chemicals methyldibromo glutaronitrile.

Feminine wipes-highly toxic chemicals, these include endocrine disrupting parabens, triclosan, synthetic fragrances and a lot more that I couldn't even pronounce (Women's Voices for the Earth,"Chem Fatale," http://www.womenvoices.org/issues/reports/chem-fatale/).

Deodorant & Antiperspirant

Deodorants were invented in 1888, with the roll-on launched in 1952 and the aerosol in 1965. An ingredient used in underarm deodorant is aluminium, a metal compound that blocks the lymphatic toxins from being removed from your body. The aluminium deposits itself into breast tissue after being absorbed into your skin. Thankfully, today you can now purchase natural deodorants without harmful ingredients.

Body Soaps & Washes

Benzyl acetate is a perfume chemical linked to liver adenomas, carcinomas, stomach tumours and pancreatic cancer. Sodium laureth sulfate damages cellular genetics and also inhibits the skin's ability to retain moisture. Check out your shampoo and conditioner it may also contain SLS that you may not even be aware of (http://www.ewg.skindeep/ingredient/706089/SODIUM_LAURETH_SULFATE_/).

Toothpaste

According to the website, fluoride is a toxic additive, an industrial waste product linked to lower IQ in children and dental fluorosis or mottling of teethFluoride *Action Network*, "New Study Challenges Old belief on Dental Fluorosis/Tooth Decay, "http://fluoridealert.org/articles/science-watch14/).

Shampoo and Conditioner

Check your shampoo and conditioner. They may contain the chemical sodium laureth sulfate that's harmful, and you may not be aware of it. Cedarwood oil is a great tonic for the hair and scalp when used as an ingredient in shampoo and conditioner.

Skin Care

Because I have always been interested in skincare and beauty products, I have adapted a good skincare routine. Applying the correct cleansers, astringents, and day and night moisturizers to my face was part of my daily ritual, although I wasn't aware of the toxic ingredients added to beauty products. As a teenager, I had very oily skin with pimples and blackheads, which was embarrassing sometimes. Just before I was going out somewhere special, a large pimple would erupt on my nose between my eyebrows. Skincare products on the market today are designed for different types of problem skins, dry, oily, and combination, but they are not necessarily beneficial.

You can purchase inexpensive and also highly priced beauty products loaded with harmful chemicals that will do more harm to your skin and will impact on your health long term.

It's also very important to drink lots of pure, clean water every day to hydrate your skin and all your organs. First thing in the morning after you wake up and before breakfast, drink at least three large glasses of filtered water with squeezed lemon juice, which helps eliminate the toxins that have been building up in your systems during sleep. The skin around your eye area is so delicately thin and does not contain many sebaceous glands. It is attached very loosely to the underlying muscles and lacks the fatty supporting tissue that is present in other areas of the face. As a result, dryness and wrinkles appear prematurely. Always dab cream lightly with your ring finger, making sure you do not drag or stretch the skin. Naturally we are always squinting and rubbing our eyes, so this is the area to show the first signs of aging.

Establish a Good Routine For acne prone skin, you would use ingredients in your products to help fight against the bacteria that clogs the pores.

Cleanser. Use a gentle, acidic cleanser, twice a day, morning and night, which leaves your skin feeling squeaky clean without striping your skin of its natural oils. Applying a gentle exfoliation mask at least twice a week is needed to cleanse at a deeper level and minimize the appearance of pores.

Toner. Next use a non alcohol toner which helps minimize pores, smooths the skins surface and help maintain the correct pH level. Cedarwood oil is a good astringent.

Day Moisturizer. The purpose of a day moisturizer is to provide a barrier between the skin and external environment. Remember: a dry atmosphere will take up water from wherever it can. Moisturizers must be replaced frequently to compensate for this. This is why it's so important to drink lots of water in your daily ritual. A day cream should hydrate, nourish, and be a protective shield from the elements like the wind, sun, pollution, central heating, and air conditioning.

Also, drinking aloe vera juice and applying the gel from the plant will help moisturize your skin.

Night Crème. When we are sleeping, the skin is the most receptive and it's the busiest time for cell repair and renewal. If you have really oily skin, you shouldn't need a moisturizer. The skin is releasing hormones such as melatonin and cortisol to repair and fight free radicals and the oxidative stress of the day.

If you're sleep deprived, this also creates more oxidative stress in the body, which interferes with the body's ability to produce collagen and elastin.

Your skin loses moisture at night, so having a layer of built-up grime, makeup, and sebum aren't really the sorts of nutrients that you skin desperately requires when the air is squeezing hydration from its surface. Never, never, ever go to sleep with your makeup left on-this will age your skin. The simplest, safest, and most effective moisturizer is pure moisturizing oils, either coconut or jojoba oils. Shea butter (also a natural sunscreen) is great, and so is sesame oil.

Most teenage skins tend to be oily or combination, because the hormones have activated into overdrive, preparing for adulthood. But this should settle down for most people in their twenties, although adult acne is possible.

Oily skins are more prone to have blackheads and pimples, and this is what's known as a problem skin. For young skin and acne-prone skin, you would use products suited especially for your skin type.

Good products to use are those that do not contain any chemicals. Harsh chemicals are toxic to your long term health and I have included a list at the end of this chapter.

Remedies for Pimple Break Out
Apple cider vinegar treatment

¼ teaspoon apple cider vinegar

1 drop of organic tea tree essential oil (great for inflamed skin)

Apply apple cider on a cottonwood bud. Add a drop of the oil to the bud and dab on the pimple. Leave on overnight. You can also use lavender essential oil if you have sensitive skin.

Aspirin and lemon juice treatment

- 3- 6 asprin
- 1-2 tablespoons fresh-squeezed lemon juice

Because aspirin contains amino salicylic, it is also a good spot treatment for pimples. Lemon juice is a citric acid with antibacterial properties, great for healing acne. You will need to crush three to six aspirin in a container. Use three if a small area or six if larger coverage is needed. Squeeze fresh lemon juice, about one tablespoon to three aspirin, and add to the aspirin to dissolve into a paste. Apply this paste to your infected pimple or all over face for a mask and allow to dry then wash off with washer with lukewarm water or baking soda.

Banana Mask for Oily Skins

- 1 ripe banana
- 2 tablespoons of honey
- 1 teaspoon of lemon juice

Mash banana and mix in honey the add lemon juiceApply to face for fifteen minutes then rinse off with face washer.

The most effective way to stop germs from spreading and pimples

Ann Carni

to develop is washing your face twice a day and keeping your hands from touching your face. Your hands touch zillions of objects every day - chairs, door-knobs, pens and waiting rooms magazines, for example. Before you apply your make-up always have your face and neck clean and don't forget to take your make-up off before you go to bed.

The Blank Canvas

Now that your skin is clean and the day moisturizer is applied, we are ready to paint your blank canvas face. Firstly, I apply a primer over my entire face and neck as it creates a flawless canvas for your makeup application. Your skin feels like velvet, minimizing open pores and fine lines. You can apply it over your eyelids to help support your eye shadow's staying power. Your foundation will last longer so you will be actually be saving time and money. Of course, it's possible to have a tinted moisturizer with sunscreen, which looks beautiful if you want something very light and natural.

Liquid foundation or mineral powder foundation

Foundation provides the back drop to your make-up and is applied to enhance or improve the natural skin colour. It should provide a smooth, even finish and protect the skin. Choose one which contains a sunscreen. Skin colours are described as pale, medium, or dark, with neutral, pink, yellow, red, or blue-tones. Skin with yellow tones is referred to as sallow or olive.

Foundation colours should be chosen to:

- Match or add warmth to neutral skin tones (golden, honey and tan shades)
- Neutralize pink or red skin tones (beige and olive shades)
- Brighten yellow or blue skin tones (rose, golden and bronze shades)

Hair colour comes into play when choosing a foundation colour, and tones of hair are usually described as ash, which is cold and neutral; golden, which is yellowish; and red, which is warm. The colour of the foundation should compensate for cold and warm tones in the hair so that there is a contrast, which adds interest to the make-up.

To test the correct colour, apply the foundation above the angle of the jaw and blend in. If it's correct. It will be a natural look and this will be the perfect canvas to start painting all the beautiful colours of eye shadows, cheek colours and lip sticks.

Mineral Powder Foundation

This is lightweight foundation, which creates a soft-focus effect, giving skin a radiant, flawless appearance.

Cosmetics

This is where you express yourself and create a dramatic, romantic, or natural look for your face.

Research has shown that woman who wear make-up look younger, earn more, and get promoted more. It's a good idea to make sure your make-up suits the time of day and the clothes you're wearing. For example, you wouldn't wear an elegant evening dress with minimal, natural makeup or wear heavy, dramatic make-up with false eye lashes going to the movies. It's best to invest in a really good set of make-up brushes. The ones made from horse hair are gentle on your skin, and to keep them in good condition, wash your brushes in shampoo and rinse well. If you are unsure of how to correctly apply your make-up, take a look at YouTube videos for advice and tips.

Enrolling in a make-up course during the school holidays at your local beauty school is always fun and educational. My cousin sent her three teenage daughters to makeup classes, and it was well worth the money. The girls can apply their makeup perfectly and know what colours will enhance their looks.

Basic Principles

Draw attention and highlight with light colours, an example use glitter on the outer corner of your eyes.

Dark colours with recede, example using smoky grey or charcoal eyeshadow. Soft and muted colours will minimize, an example use pale, pink matte lipstick. To emphasize use bright and clear colours an example would be using bright, glossy red lipstick. Your cosmetic kit will consist of blushes, foundation, primer, bronzes, eye shadows, lip liners, lipsticks, lip gloss, eye liners, powders, mascara and glitter highlighters all to your liking and colour pallet. A blusher is the most highly pigmented contour cosmetic; therefore, it has the greatest effect. Use it over the prominent parts of your face.

Caring for your Brushes

Our make-up brushes need to be cleaned regularly so you don't spread oil and germs to your skin. Once a month, give your brushes a good clean with hair shampoo and water, rinse with lukewarm water, and then allow to dry. I also clean my hair brushes this way, and remember: don't rinse your brushes in hot water.

Nasty Chemicals Used in Beauty Products

- Animal products or animal by-products
- Parabens, a preservative used in many moisturizes and cosmetics
- Formaldehyde, a releasing preservative (usually for embalming people) DMDM hydantoin, diazolidinyl urea, imidazolidinyl urea, methenamine, and uarternium-15are used in a variety of cosmetics

- Mineral oil, derived from petrol and used as a spreading agent and is the cheapest form of oil on the planet and an indefinite shelf life.
- Petroleum jelly used for shine in some hair products and in many phthalateslip balms, lipsticks and moisturizers.
- *S*odium lauryl sulphate used to create foam in products such as shampoos, cleansers and bubble baths
- Coal tar dyes used in hair dyes and coloured makeup
- Dibutyl phthalate used as a plasticiser in some nail care *products*
- Partum (fragrance) artificial ingredients are used in many cosmetics and beauty productsxcvnm,./
- Siloxanes, silicon-based chemicals used to soften, smooth and moisten many cosmetics, hair products and deodorant creams.
- Triclosan, an antibacterial included in products such as toothpaste, cleansers and antiperspirant (http://www.medusasmakeup.com/history-of-makeup.htm)

Buy your beauty products that are either certified organic, chemical-free, or botanical–based. That way you're saying no to the companies that supply nasty chemicals that are compromising your health. Each one of us deserves harmless ingredients in the products we buy, ingredients that are beneficial to our skin, hair, and teeth. Let these companies who are cheating us know we are standing up against their big profits at the expense of our health. Just don't hand over your money-be a voice to be heard.

My mum always said, "Look your best, because you never know who you might meet," and I think that's good advice.

CHAPTER 11

GIRLS JUST WANT TO HAVE FUN

Whenever someone in my family said he or she was bored, my mum would give them a job to do, so we soon learnt to keep our mouths zipped. Boredom is dull, uneventful, feeling stuck, mopping around, which equals to being unproductive. We all need a balanced life and to plan our time wisely, to schedule in activities that are fun and those that we don't enjoy but necessary so we won't be bored.

I always looked forward to our holiday road trips, to see new places and experience new things, driving to the Blue Mountains, the Gold Coast, and Ballarat, Victoria. Australia is a beautiful, fascinating country. Travelling by road is advisable if you're travelling short distances or have a lot of time. This country is big, with diverse landscapes, so flying is better, as it will take you four hours to fly from Sydney across to Perth, for instance. It's very different for kids now, travelling by plane interstate and overseas with affordable holiday packages or cruising the high seas on ocean liners, stopping at various ports along the way.

Most teens have probably been lucky enough to have travelled to the big theme parks in Queensland, Movie World, Sea World, Dream World, White Water World, and Magic Mountain, if you live on the east coast of Australia. And there's also the Australian outback adventure, Currumbin Wildlife Sanctuary, IFly Indoor Skydiving, TreeTop Challenge, and Australia Zoo for entertainment. Treasure all the memories with your family if you have had the opportunity to go on holidays, even if it's camping or caravanning. And just for the record, I love these holidays. Where else can you see millions of stars right across the sky and snuggle up around a camp fire? Or how about going to the snowfields in winter and learning to snowboard or ski?

Girlfriends having Fun in the Snow
Photo @Dragos Daniel Illiescu/Dreamtime.com

If, for a number of reasons, you haven't been on any holidays other than school camp, then choosing your own exciting adventures when you're older will be fun. I didn't go on an overseas holiday till I was thirty-eight years old, and then I wondered why I hadn't planned to go earlier.

If you travel overseas, always have travel insurance. There have even been instances where travellers have extended their holiday stays but forgotten to extend the insurance. Don't make that mistake.

Your life growing up as a teenager will be very different than mine. You will have more opportunities and more adventures. When I was growing up, my family always celebrated bonfire night in our backyard with our neighbours. For weeks, my two elder brothers, Peter and Glenn, with their mates would gather tree branches to build a huge bonfire that looked much like an Indian tee pee. It stood tall and wide, and when it was well alight, you were warmed by the glowing, hot flames. The amber colours danced before your eyes, mesmerizing you with its soft glow. Mum would supply unskinned potatoes wrapped in foil and placed these in the fire to be cooked. When the potatoes were cooked and slightly cooled, they were cut and eaten with a dollop of butter.

Bonfire night was to celebrate the birthday of the British monarch, Queen Elizabeth II, and was usually held on the long weekend in June. You were allowed to have fireworks back when I was a teenager, but now the government has banned them in most states because people were getting seriously injured. Firecrackers were of different varieties such as sparklers, tom thumbs, tuppeny bungers, double bungers, sky rockets, and pinwheels. The boys liked the firecrackers that made loud, noises and skyrockets that shot high in the air.

The morning after, you could see a huge, black, burnt circle on the ground that was once dad's lawn, but he never seemed to mind at all. He always said it was just grass and would grow back.

We always enjoyed the RSL (Returned Service League) annual picnic. This was held early in the year around February, down Easts Beach in Kiama on the South Coast, with its lush, green open spaces surrounded by shaded trees around the perimeter. And, of course, the beautiful sandy beach to build sand sculptures and clear, aqua-coloured rolling waves to body surf and swim. Each family packed their own picnic food, but all the mums baked family favourites of cakes and slices to share around. The main feature was the cricket match, with every man, woman, and child having a turn of batting and bowling, and this would last most of the day. We also had running, sack, piggyback, skipping, and relay races for different age groups, with the adults joining in as well. There was a reward of a chocolate bar for the first three place-getters getters at the finish line, but at the end, nobody missed out with a surprise of a lolly bag.

Piggy Back Races
Photo @Signorina/Dreamtime.com

And, of course, there were Christmas parties, church picnics, school and church fetes, fashion parades, Saturday afternoon movies, and the annual Easter show and agricultural show. We enjoyed walking along the farm paddocks at the back of our home during blackberry season and picking fresh berries to make pies. Most Sundays, mum cooked the Sunday roast, and later, Dad took the car out for a Sunday drive with a treat of an ice-cream afterwards.

You don't need to have a lot of money to have fun. Your community entertainment with street fairs and musical entertainment is all free. Take a picnic lunch with you when you go down to the beach, park, or swimming pool. Watch the local footy match, go for a bike ride, or hang around with your girlfriends, dancing and singing with your favourite music. Maybe you love to read books. The local library has a huge range of travel books, and you can travel the world in the comfort of your favourite chair. If history, fiction, nonfiction, photography, art, sewing, biographies, fashion, and inventions take your fancy, then the library will have it.

What do adolescents today do for fun? You love to party, hang around with all your friends at the movies and shopping malls, or listen to your favourite music. Technology is so advanced it's hard to keep up with all the latest media equipment you can buy today. You can purchase the latest gadget, and six months later companies will bring out a newer model that's better and faster. The most necessary item for an adolescent today is your smartphone, which you constantly use. Television and gaming consoles with PlayStation 4 and Wii are popular with you.

The average teen is very tech savvy and spends eleven hours in front of screens every day. That's a huge chunk out of your day. The apps you like are Snapchat for communicating with your friends, and Spotify is your best music app. PokemonGo is the app game that has you trying to capture Pokemon monsters, train them, and put them into battle against other players. The advantages are you actually have to walk or drive to real-life locations and meet others, so you're socializing and exercising, although there is the danger of some sinister person knowing your whereabouts. And people have been looking at the app when they have been walking or driving and have had unfortunate accidents and injuries.

You like sharing your funny pictures with Instagram, and for quick updates, you like Twitter better than Facebook. You're not on FB as much as your parents and friends' parents, because you feel you can't say or be yourself. Facebook maybe dead to you, but the cool thing you like about FB is you can text your friends through FB messenger.

Television is cool if you have cable and streaming services, and Netflix is a popular as there is no commercials.

Millions of teens also use the After school app, a social network specifically created for high school students.

This is where they post their deepest thoughts, anxieties, secret crushes, vulgar assessments of their classmates, and even violent threats.

Musical.Ly is Apple's newest app lets you make music videos of yourself or other people. And teens are obsessed with the Japanese game called Neko Atsume, where you collect cats, literally online.

Avoid being pressured into doing harmful acts, like harming other people, property, possessions, or animals. Never write anything that will cause you to be seen as unkind or disrespectful to others.

Remember: a potential employer may be looking at your post updates and not like what they see or read.

CHAPTER 12

* * * * * * * * * * * * * * * *

THE INTERNET AND PREDATORS

R ecently I watched an Australian television program on channel
SBS that exposed some scrupulous characters on an online
dating service.

There's nothing wrong with meeting others on the Internet and
wanting to find friendship and love relationships in your life. With
the high rate of break-ups and divorces, if you are a single parent, it
is the perfect way to meet up. You sign up to the website, forward a
photo of yourself, your likes, and some personal details, and stream
for your perfect match. Then you scroll through the list, finding a
person of similar, age, and tastes, someone you think you would like
to meet. Of course, you have no Idea if the person you are meeting
is genuine or trustworthy.

On the program, under the watchful eye of a specialized police
team, all activity was scrutinized to catch a possible predator. The
police for several weeks had been watching the activity of several
males on the dating site who'd befriended single mothers with
teenage daughters.

A woman police officer posing as a single mum with a young
fifteen- year-old daughter started chatting with one of the males on
the dating site. After exchanging conversations and photographs, it
was obvious the predator had a keen interest in the mum's young

fifteen-year-old adolescent daughter. As the conversations progressed, confidently the man asked if it was possible if they could have a threesome together. The predator lived in Melbourne, and he would arrange all flights and accommodation for mum and the daughter over the weekend, and he would meet them at the airport. It was all arranged, and when the police knew it was the correct man who identified himself after meeting the woman and the young teenager at the airport, the police seized him. He was taken down to the police station and later charged with unlawfully perpetrating to have sex with a minor under the age of sixteen years. Later in court, the man was charged guilty, and he is now serving eight years' jail term with the hope that he can be rehabilitated.

Apparently this is a special division of the police force, and they carefully watch for sexual predators.

Sexual predators can be living in your neighbourhood and will try and befriend you on any social media sites such as Facebook or Pinterest.

A lot of times men will identify themselves as teenage boys, having fake portrait photos on their profiles, and you harmlessly accept their friend requests.

On the Lookout for Internet Predators
Photo @Olga Donskaya/Dreamtime.com

123

He has checked out your profile, your posts, and sneakily charms you over the next few weeks. He wants to meet you, as he is coming to your town and arranges to meet you at a public place of your choosing, knowing full well both your parents are working.

Once you agree and you go to the meeting place, you will find he is a middle-aged man, nothing like his picture. Don't be charmed with his words. Don't whatsoever leave the premises with him. Make some excuse and go to the bathroom if they have one, seek help from other diners, call your parents or a relative to come pick you up, and phone the police. You have just had a close encounter with a sexual predator, and this time you were lucky.

Another television program I was watching did an experiment and asked the parents if their teenage daughters knew about stranger danger. Of course, they all said yes, so the test was to find out what would happen if a stranger befriended their children. At first, the man befriended a fourteen-year-old daughter on the Internet, and the parents knew exactly what was happening. After a few weeks, the stranger asked his new friend if she wanted to come over to his place and look at his new puppy. The child agreed and the man asked her if she wanted him to pick her up at home. He already knew her parents weren't at home, as they were working, and she agreed.

It was all secretly filmed, and the parents watched it all unfold on a surveillance camera, horrified to find out that their daughter actually walked out the house and walked away with the stranger to his car. Luckily, it was all set up and arranged for television viewing, but it shows me that we have to be diligent in reinforcing stranger danger. It's easy to be distracted and refrain from common sense. If something doesn't feel right or you are doing something secretly, then warning bells are ringing.

What if you know the sleaze and he is a close family friend, relative, or your stepfather? Never allow anyone to ever touch you on any part of your body if you don't want them to.

Sometimes they are so sneaky that you are not even aware of it happening. A little brush against your breasts, a pat on the bum, or a rub on your thigh as you walk past them. I remember sitting next to a male friend at a private gathering, and we were engaged in conversation when I felt something on my leg. As I looked down, I was horrified to find his hand was resting on my knee. Maybe it was a few seconds, but he did move his hand away. I quickly ended the talk, moved away, and never spoke to him again after that incident. I guess I could have made a scene, but I also noticed his wife watching out of the corner of my eye.

Perhaps this was normal behaviour for him, or he was looking for a cheap thrill, but I wasn't having a bar of it. Never allow anyone to touch you indecently, bully, intimidate, or think they have control over you. If it's blatantly obvious, stand up for yourself and look the weasel straight in the eyes and say with conviction, "I am not afraid of you, and if you ever touch me ever again I'll kick you in the groin." That should have him running for cover. He'll be too embarrassed to look at you. Use whatever words you like - don't be afraid. This will give you back your power. And if he doesn't get the message, then you must tell Mum, Dad, or someone you trust, that you feel uncomfortable with this person's behaviour and actions.

Of course, sometimes the person you tell may not believe you at first, or they may consider that it's not such a big deal, and you should just forget about it. Or they may consider that you're trying to cause trouble or making up lies just get attention. Remember, also: the person you have told could be in shock if they know the culprit and they are trying to process through this distressing information. Be as open and true to the facts as you possibly can and find a safe house where you can stay for a couple of days. Approach the person you have told again for another meeting so appropriate action can be carried out.

When you aren't given a satisfactory outcome, then you as the innocent victim need to consider your next steps.

1. It can be sexual suggestions or sexual remarks making you feel unworthy, so therefore, always avoid his or her company or being alone with that person.
2. If they have sexually abused or raped you, go to the police immediately.

If they threaten you with death threats, go to the police or authorities immediately.

Always seek professional counselling after you have been through a traumatic experience. While you are powerless to control or change other people, you do have the power to disassociate with people who abuse you, are consistently negative, expose you to dangerous circumstances, or who tell you who you should be rather than supporting the best of who you are.

Warning

The Internet comes with plenty of good websites but also some bad ones. One of the website I'm speaking of is recruiting young adolescents and grooming them for terrorist attacks anywhere in the world. How distressing it must be for a parent to find out his or her adolescent daughter or son didn't arrive at their planned holiday destination and later finding out they were in a foreign country being trained and groomed as human suicide bombers! How is it possible that innocent people are being brainwashed into this activity by some magical power? How tragic and distressing to be told later that your child is dead, a suicide bomber.

And why are adolescents lured into homosexuality through websites by powerful, rich men promising their victims lots of cash just to fulfil their lusty, secretive needs?

Maybe the innocent victim's life is spiralling out of control. Many die from drug overdose from a drug habit or suicide through guilt and shame. I wish I had all the answers to comfort and protect these wonderful young adolescents, and my heart aches for the victims and families.

My prayer is that those who are vulnerable and are reading this book is to contact the helpline in your state.

Popular games on the Internet

- Call of Duty
- Halo Reach
- Minecraft
- Clash of Clans
- Club Penguin
- Age of Empires Online
- Eve Online
- Far Cry
- Battlefield
- Red Dead Redemption
- World of Warcraft
- Free Realms

Minecraft is probably the most popular video game, because people find it macho. The cartoony characters, animals, and monsters look innocent when compared to the graphic images contained in so many other games. But don't be deceived: Minecraft isn't some child's play game. It can be additive and quite violent. Players attack and kill other players and steal their hard-earned (or bought) virtual possessions, or destroy the buildings they have worked hard to build. Server owners can sell special packages of tools, weapons, armour, and other accessories to players on their servers, which is very tempting.

I have known kids to spend many hundreds of dollars this way, often stealing their parents' credit card numbers to pay for their Minecraft purchases. Minecraft does have positive qualities, however. It's an incredible medium for creative expression. Some have described Minecraft as "LEGO on steroids." The bottom line is to have fun. It's wonderful to play games that allow you think with imagination, but be careful you don't get sucked in with spending all your time playing and spending unnecessary money. Set boundaries around playing any game online. Only play for a reasonable amount of time and play with friends you know, not strangers. Your parents want to trust you. Don't give them any reason not to. Honesty is the best policy. There have been incidents where total strangers have conned innocent players into giving personal computer information and have hacked money from accounts (http://challengingboys. com/2015/05/4-tips-to-keep-kids-safe-on-minecraft/).

CHAPTER 13

· ◦ ※ ◦ ● ◦ ● ● ● ● ● ◦ ● ◦ ● ◦ ◦ ※

SETTING BOUNDARIES

Your self-worth can be greatly enhanced by setting boundaries on how you allow other people to treat you. A boundary is like a fence that pens a herd of cattle, and that's what we do by setting a boundary to protect and take care of us, just like the cattle. Boundaries lets others know you respect and value yourself and you have guidelines of what you will not or will tolerate in someone's behaviour. If you don't, then you leave yourself open for anger, resentment, or attack. Setting boundaries for yourself is important for self-respect and worthiness. We can also define this as admiration, confidence, and kindness. We see these qualities in others but we don't think we are worthy enough to possess these characteristics for ourselves. We put ourselves down by being negative and put others up on a pedestal, meanwhile short-changing ourselves.

Clearly communicating your boundaries lets others know your availability, values, needs, feelings, and rights, and this establishes positive, healthy relationships. You set boundaries to change yourself, not the other person-it's none of your business their behaviour. You will have more self-respect when you demonstrate your boundaries, but it's not about control or manipulation of the other person.

Ann Carni

Setting Clear Boundaries will help Build Your Confidence
Photo @ Glenda Powers/Dreamtime.com

Feeling Lighter

Your surroundings inside and outside the home are important to your health, success, and joy?

Just the simple changers of decluttering, cleaning, and moving the furniture around can have a positive effect on your life. When you start eliminating the dirt and junk from your bedroom, car, or surroundings, you start allowing that stuck energy to circulate raising your energy. From this lighter feeling comes new ideas and clearer thinking, which will become evident as the weeks go by. You honestly won't even care about the small stuff anymore, and as this becomes a habit, you will be able to manage the big challenges.

Anyway, cleaning your room shows respect for yourself and respect for your parents if you're living at home. It shows you care about your belongings and lets others know that you are worthy enough to receive more material blessings. And don't allow others to abuse your stuff like being disrespectful and not returning borrowed goods in A1 condition.

Let's start talking about your relationships, and I want you to write down anything that you would consider inappropriate behaviour or annoying to you.

Identify the people in your life who deplete your energy and who are draining. The people in your life who gossip or belittle you or others. Identify those people who don't support you in your activities or work. When you have identified those people who don't have your best interests at heart. Ask yourself, "Can I stop seeing these people?" If these people are family, maybe you could switch off to their unwelcome words or possibly don't see them as much.

Eliminate other people's issues; they are none of your business. Anyone who is negative to you and influences you in such a way is domineering and not wanting you to change and better yourself.

These people are sabotaging you and not allowing you to become your true, authentic self.

But you know what's worse? It's self-sabotage, that little voice in your head saying"You're not good enough to become a doctor. You wouldn't last the distance in studying for years. You like to party, remember? Just get a job, go out, and meet a boy, get married, have some kids, be supported financially, and never have to work again. So what's the point on studying and becoming a doctor?"

"What's the point to eating healthy and going to the gym, doing weight lifting, going bike riding, and nearly killing yourself in the process? Mum and Dad are both overweight. I'm the same build, and all my family are huge. It's hereditary. Look I'm probably going to get diabetes, arthritis, and hypertension anyway, and they just take prescription medication to help relieve their ailments. I'll just pop some pills also when I need to, and for now, I'll skip the gym and have a piece of chocolate mud cake with ice cream."

If you are either one of these people, do you think you will be really healthy or happy with your life in twenty or thirty years' time?

If you have a dream inside of you, you deserve the same respect and worthiness you give others. Never allow anyone to control you, and by this, I will explain. There is a certain standard in society that we need to observe. There are rules and regulations that need to be upheld by law. For instance, we can't barge into a courtroom session while proceedings are on, or we will be in contempt of court by the magistrate. If you're yelling and screaming obscenities, the judge will have you arrested and lock you up in a police cell. You can't go through red lights or go over the speed limit on roads without getting a traffic infringement notice.

This is control, but it's for your protection and the protection of others. The control I'm talking about is someone manipulating or using tactics to get you to do something that you don't want to do or stopping you from doing something. For instance, let's say you have just had a huge argument with your boyfriend or husband. You can see that if you continue much longer in their company you will probably say or do something that you might regret. So the wisest option is to leave the house, either by grabbing your car keys or going for a walk.

If your partner grabs the keys from you or out of the ignition or deadlocks the doors to stop you from leaving, this is controlling behaviour. I'm not sure if you are aware, but your boyfriend can't hold you hostage, it's against the law. The only exception would be if you were intoxicated, had taken drugs, or had over self-medicated yourself and you were a danger to yourself and others, such as driving a car.

A Good Night's Sleep

Many of us do not enjoy a good night's sleep. We either have difficulty in falling asleep or staying asleep for eight to ten hours of sleep. If we awaken through the night, we toss and turn, and when we finally manage to get back to sleep, the alarm clock sounds, time to get up.

Understanding the causes of Insomnia

- Bright lights from street lights entering through sheer bedroom curtains
- Watching television and using computers or social media too near bedtime
- Consuming too many caffeinated products, soda drinks, coffee or chocolate throughout the day
- Consuming recreational drugs like alcohol
- Bedroom too warm or stuffy
- Bedclothes too warm or cool for the season
- You're snoring loudly and it wakes you up
- You are in pain or have a sickness, such as the flu, and find it difficult to breathe
- Your mind is too active - you just can't switch off
- Stressing about an issue you have no control over or an upcoming exam or report that's due tomorrow

In Search of a Good Night's Sleep

Some of the causes are simple to rectify:

- Check to make sure your bedroom is completely dark, perhaps using block-out blinds or curtains.
- Don't have any electrical devices, such as a TV, in your bedroom.
- Try not to watch action or violent movies, which cause too much brain stimulation before bedtime.
- Don't drink after 8:00 p.m. and certainly not caffeinated drinks before bedtime.
- Don't go to bed on a full stomach. Finish eating at least two hours before going to bed. Your digestive system is trying to assimilate your food.

- Abstain from recreational drugs. If you admit you need help, seek help.
- Your bedroom should be a slightly cooler temperature. Open your window to avoid stuffiness or use ceiling fans on a warm night.
- Make sure your mattress and pillow is comfortable and bed clothes not too heavy.

Sickness can be a problem if it's a chronic illness, like asthma. I suffered from chronic sinus problems with swollen nasal passages, which can cause sleepless nights. Chronic pain is difficult to deal with physiologically and physically, and I know your doctor will insist you use pain medication and sometimes prescription sleeping tablets. Drug companies warn in the fine print that sleeping pills are intended to be used for seven to ten days only and not for long periods. These drugs are habit forming and cause side effects such as memory loss, dizziness, and drowsiness and coordination difficulties. There are over-the-counter sleep remedies, but they are still not for extended use. If your mind is overthinking the everyday issues of work, school, or extracurricular activities, or even over money issues, then it's hard to have a good night's sleep. Ask yourself, "How can I simplify my life?" Life can get pretty busy; maybe the pressure is too much.

Are we overcommitting and expecting too much of ourselves? Sometimes we just need to stop and rethink of what we're doing and ask ourselves, "Is this how I want to really live and can I change my circumstances now or in the near future?" Just reassessing the situation, we can get a clearer picture in our heads of what's really going on. Look, if you can't change anything, then look for ways you can cope better- a relaxing bath, light yoga or meditation before bedtime. Spending fifteen minutes writing a list of ten things you are grateful for and write down three things you want to achieve tomorrow is effective

If you have a problem and need answers, ask God or the universe to help solve the issue and then let it go. If you are feeling fear in trying something new and difficult or it's scary, I think you should congratulate yourself instead. Fear can be a healthy sign that you are stretching yourself into new territory and out of your comfort zone. It means you are reaching down inside yourself to find the resources, wisdom, and conviction that you will need to succeed. Somewhere along the line we have the idea that if we felt fear, it was a bad thing and a signal to stop in our tracks. Making a decision that scares us and not having it turn out the way we wanted may shake our confidence level but nobody's life is in danger.

Deciding to back away from growth because it feels scary and uncomfortable is a mistake. The bad news is that, the next time you face something that makes you feel afraid, it will be even tougher.

At school your choice of elective subjects will most likely lead you into the career that you want to pursue. If you choose subjects you feel you would like, then you will be more eager to learn. The friendships you form in these formative years can be life-changing and bring about long-lasting friendships. Your choice of work or career can change many times over the course of your working life for a variety of reasons. You may have been forced to have a career change because of illness, disability, being sacked, retrenched or moving to another state or country. Change is inevitable, nothing can stay the same, and you learn and grow. Your choice of partner may change over the years. Your ideals and philosophy may change as you grow older.

You are still young and there is so much for you to discover in life, most of your dreams are still to be fulfilled.

> Optimism is the faith that leads to achievement.
> Nothing can be done without hope and confidence.
>
> Helen Keller

Ann Carni

Being Homeless

Homelessness can be defined as a loss of security, stability, privacy, and safety. Homelessness is caused by poverty. There isn't enough housing to accommodate people on low incomes and welfare payments.

It's not caused by mental illness, choice, disability, substance abuse, losing contact with family, etc. However, these things can all create poverty, which leads to homelessness. Being addicted to something, like substance abuse, makes you poor, you eventually can't work and then can't afford to pay your bills, ending with an eviction notice from the landlord. We all need access to safe housing. Sleeping rough on the streets or under makeshift dwelling can be dangerous. Sleeping on a friend's couches, caravans, squats, and refuges is temporary but isn't the solution, and two out of three people who look for crisis accommodation are turned away. Homelessness is traumatic and is often the end point to a series of life events and family breakdowns. You and your parents or carers have relationship problems, so you want to leave home. Staying at school longer to obtain a good education can increase your chances of obtaining suitable employment, and this is, after all, a competitive world. If you live in a home where your parents are unemployed, it's time to break the poverty cycle.

Help comes from many groups and one successful program. The Detour Program in Victoria is in partnership with three agencies that offers an early- intervention program designed to stop a young person from leaving home, if it is safe to do so. After the young person is interviewed by the counsellor and still wants to leave home, then a mediation meeting is set up. All parties - the counsellor, parents or carers, and you - if agreed, set up rules to live by. A demountable studio is installed by Kids Under Cover in the parent's rear yard of the home or a relative's. This way the young person is able to go to school and be educated.

There are 105,000 people in Australia without homes, and it is a national disgrace that we are not taking more action to end homelessness. One in twenty Indigenous Australians are without homes, and 75 percent live in overcrowded dwellings. Northern Territory has the highest rate in the country, at fifteen times the national average.

Children aged under eighteen years account for nearly 30 percent of the countries homeless population, and nearly 20 percent are aged under twelve years.

These figures are appalling, so what can we do to address this situation?

- The youth of today have higher unemployment than any other age group. So staying in school longer, getter a better education for a good job, is a major part of the solution.
- The government needs to provide more teachers and free fees for higher education and provide more opportunities for work skills and trades.
- Youth in rural and remote areas need more job prospects, giving farmers and retail storekeepers more money grants with an incentive to employ the local youth for work.
- Domestic violence and physical and mental abuse are big issues in our society as well as boredom, lack of money, and poor self-esteem.

Living in Australian cities housing has become too expensive to buy, with rental properties in demand and unaffordable for a person on welfare benefits. So with a shortage of housing, it's become almost a disgrace to see renters being exploited by shameful landlords renting their high-priced units or homes with appalling living standards.

Domestic violence is the single biggest cause of homelessness in Australia.When I was a young, married mother with two small children, I was a victim of domestic violence by my first husband. It wasn't an ideal way to live, and I virtually walked on eggshells during this time.

In his defence, he was a good provider and never abused the children physically, and I stayed in the marriage for a number of years. Friends told me to leave the marriage, but I didn't, because I thought he would change and things would get better and unfortunately, that's not how the fairy tale ended. Eventually I lost my self-worth and confidence, and then I lost respect for him. I have omitted to tell you all the details, but the police witnessed enough of the situation and advised me to leave and go to a women's refuge centre.

Feeling numb and unemotional, it was hard trying to be a caring mum, but somehow we all coped. I had counselling sessions with the social worker, who asked for all the painful details of my marriage. My children had other children to play with, as I wasn't the only mother living in a women's refuge for safety reasons. Eventually my feelings surfaced, and I felt angry, embarrassed, humiliated, degraded, and ashamed for being in that situation.

I didn't think I deserved to be there, and when I think of homelessness, I often think of the old man sleeping on a park bench with an empty bottle of wine. The only reason I tell this story is for you to see that you have choices in life and whatever choices you make then you live with your decisions.

The only advice to give you is, if ever anyone hits, punches, kicks, pushes, or verbally belittles and abuses you, run and keep running. There are billions of people in the world who you haven't even met. You'll find people who are caring and loving who want to see you happy. No one can tell you what to do about your life. You will know in your own time to make the right decision and only then.

Contact Names and Numbers if You Need Help:

- 000 in immediate danger
- 1800Respect 24/7 sexual assault, domestic and violence counselling services 1800737732,www.1800respect.org.au

- Link2Home provides information, conducts assessments, as well as makes referrals to homelessness services across NSW, 24/7,1800825855
- Victoria 1800825955 outside business hours will be directed to Salvation Army Crisis Services
- Queensland 1800811811 or emergency housing TTY: 1800812-225 or phone for homeless
- Single people over sixteen years, mothers with children 1800474753 (1800 HPIQLD) or TTY 1800010222, www. qld.gov.au/homelesshotline
- Western Australia (08) 94425777
- South Australia Youth fifteen- twenty-five years 1800807364 or homeless gateway 1800003308
- Northern Territory ShelterMe Directory, www.shelterme. org.au/
- Tasmania 1800800588 24/7

You may apply for rental assistance by obtaining one of the following:

- Bond Assistance Loan
- Commonwealth Rent Assistance
- The National Rental Affordability Scheme
- Private Rental Aboriginal Assistance Loan
- Remote Aboriginal Housing
- Social Housing (community and pub)

CHAPTER 14

DRIVING LICENSES

One of the most exciting thrills you will experience as a teenager is obtaining your driving license. There is nothing like getting behind the wheel of the car all alone, cruising down the road. Your heart will be pumping with the rush of adrenaline. And as you gain more confidence driving, it will become second nature to automatically know which pedals to push, which gears to change, and all the other controls on how and when to use unless you have an automatic.

Remember when you first sat in the driver's seat as a learner, how terrified you felt? Panic was etched on your face, and you thought you would never get the hang of it. Your brain was overloaded with new things to learn, trying to figure out the correct position of your hands on the steering wheel and how to proceed to do a reverse park or a three-point turn.

A good option is to have a few driving lessons by a qualified driving instructor. It is well worth the investment. Having the right information ensures you don't pick up any bad habits and ensures you have complete control of the car.

Always remember that a car is a fine-tuned piece of machinery that enables you to get from point A to point B. Having complete control of your car and obeying the road rules allows you to arrive at your destination in safety to yourself and others.

When I was a learner driver, I was supervised by my boyfriend at the time, and I crashed his car with considerably damage. I lost control of the car whilst negotiating around a bend. I panicked and placed my foot on the accelerator instead of the brake and ploughed into some shrubbery between two trees. We were very fortunate that nobody was hurt, although my pride was shaken up considerably.

The car wasn't a write-off, but his insurance company stated they would not cover the insurance if there was an accident whilst I was driving his car. Consequently, the police were involved, and I received notification to attend a compulsory driving lecture organized by the police force, and I was to be accompanied by a parent. Imagine my embarrassment when I arrived on the night to find I was the only girl amongst twenty other males in the room. It actually turned out to be the most informative lecture I attended about road safety, and I have no doubt that this same information is taught in all high schools around Australia.

There was a couple of things that really stuck in my mind that night, one being, even though you have the right-of-way in traffic, don't press the point. The object is to avoid an accident always. And don't assume everyone will do the right thing and follow the road rules. I see many P-plate drivers and even experienced drivers empowered to express their road rights, but seriously, who wants their car off the road at the panel repair shop, not to mention being injured? Yes, the road rules are to be adhered to at all times, but we are only human - we lose concentration and we make mistakes.

And sometimes they are costly, with loss of lives and life-threatening injuries that can result in permanent damage. The worst is knowing and not observing the road rules that result in unnecessarily accidents, such as driving without a seat-belt, driving under the influence of alcohol, or drug abuse. Applying makeup or fixing your hair, adjusting the GPS, and texting are all distractions that can cause accidents. A little common sense and maturity is

Ann Carni

what's required. If you're always running late for appointments, try to manage your time better instead of speeding.

Obtaining the Credentials

Getting your driving license won't be as simple as you might think. Just driving for a few months, and then turning up for your road test isn't easy, as you are about to find out.

Getting your L-Plates

Firstly, you will need to be the minimum age of sixteen years, and you will need to pass the Driver Knowledge Test. So obtain and read the Road Uses' Handbook and check out the Driver License Section on the Roads and Maritime website.

You can book your license test online or by phoning 132213 or going in person at any registry or service centre.

You will need proof of identification or a passport, proof of signature, and address. A payment is required, and you will have to do an eye test.

When you pass, congratulations, because this is when it gets really interesting.

You will be issued with a set of L-plates and a learner driver logbook, which is also your guidebook, and you are required to write down over 120 hours at least of driving time.

The L-plates are valid for five years and are displayed on the outside front and rear of the vehicle at all times while you're learning to drive.

Your driving instructor must supervise you at all times and can be a qualified driving instructor, parent, or other driver as long as they all have a full Australian license. The driving supervisor and you must wear a seat belt, and it is illegal for you both to be affected by alcohol or drugs while driving, attempting to drive, or instructing.

Watch out for foods containing alcohol, over-the-counter

medications, and even cough meds that could affect your concentration, mood, coordination, or reactions while driving.If you are involved in an accident and someone is taken to hospital, you will be required to produce a blood sample for drug testing.

You must not accumulate more than four demerit points, or you will need to sit for your learner's license again.

Restrictions are in place to see if you are mature enough to handle the road rules.

- 0.0 percent alcohol limit
- Maximum speed limit 90 km/h
- Not tow any vehicle
- Not use a mobile phone, not even a hands-free one, so leave it in your handbag

If you meet the requirements and are ready for the next step, you can apply for your driving license test. You will need to be seventeen years old and have been a learner driver for twelve months, with at least 120 hours of driving with a supervised driver.

Book in for your driving test and check out the requirements and helpful hints that you need to do on the Maritime and Road Service website.

On the day you will need to make sure your vehicle is immaculately clean, has roadworthy tires with correct pressure, and that everything is functioning correctly.

Dress neatly and appropriately and wear closed-in, covered shoes. You'd be surprised how many get this wrong.

Red P-Plates

Congratulations! You passed the drivers' test and can display the two red P-plates on the outside on the front and back of your car with pride for the next 12 months.

Your Restrictions

- Always remember 0.0 percent alcohol consumption
- Do not accumulate no more than four demerit points
- Maximum speed limit 90 km/h
- Not supervise a learner driver
- Not use a mobile phone or hands-free one
- Maximum towing capacity is 250 kilos
- If under twenty-five years, must not drive more than one passenger under twenty-one years between 11:00 p.m. and 5:00 a.m.
- If you obtained a manual license, you can only drive a manual car
- Not drive a vehicle with eight or more cylinders
- Driving a turbo or super charged car (diesel engine exempt) is not allowed. Making modifications to a car, or any other vehicle that increases performance is also not allowed
- Make sure you and your passengers are wearing seat belts whilst driving

Green P-Plates

Your requirements

- Hold red P-plates for twelve months
- Pass Hazard Perception Test
- Proudly display your green on white P-plates on the front and rear outside vehicle
- Not accumulate more than seven demerit points
- Wearing seat belts for driver and passengers is compulsory

Your restrictions

- 0.0 percent alcohol
- Not supervise a learner driver

- Maximum speed limit 100 km/h
- Not drive certain prohibited vehicles
- No mobile phones, nor hands free
- Not drive a vehicle 8 or more cylinders
- Driving a turbo or super charged car (diesel engine exempt) is not allowed. Making modifications to a car, or any other vehicle that increases performance is also not allowed

Full License
Your Requirements

- Hold your green P-plates for 24 months
- Pass Driver Qualification Test
- Not accumulate more than 12 demerit points
- Driver and passengers must wear seat belts

Restrictions

- 0.05 percent alcohol limit
- Maximum speed 110 km/h
- Not use a mobile phone while driving but a hands free one is acceptable

Congratulations on a job well done because you proved to yourself and others that you are responsible and trustworthy to handle the road rules. Now that you have a full license, I hope that you enjoy many years of driving throughout your life. Always remember you're sitting in a lethal machine that has the potential to maim and kill if you don't drive according to the road rules or road conditions.

The driving laws are in-force for your protection and others, you may think you look cool driving like a car-racing driver through the streets of suburbia, but actually you're a menace to society.

And sooner or later you'll be caught with a traffic infringement, loss of license, or worse, a tragic accident. There are plenty of young persons buried in the cemeteries and paraplegics or quadriplegics with shattered dreams, fighting to survive one day at a time, with months or years of pain and rehabilitation. Just imagine what it would be like for your family not to have the privilege of watching you grow into a beautiful, happy young woman if suddenly you were in an induced coma or dead.

Open your eyes and feel the heartache of pain to those families whose lives have changed because of automobile accidents. If you don't believe me, then visit a rehabilitation unit or hospital for a day and see how families and medical staff handle and respond to the pressures that are an everyday occurrence. Every year, thousands of people are involved in car accidents, through drink driving, speeding, negligence, falling asleep at the wheel. Don't let it be you or one of your friends. Be responsible and mature. Just because you have your driving license, it doesn't make you queen of the road. Be smart in keeping your driving license. It's taken you a lot of time and money.

As my husband says when he sees a driver speeding, "He or she must have a lot of money, because he or she obviously can afford to part with his or her hard earned cash with a speeding fine." If they do get caught-and it is only a matter of time- they will be fined and could possibly lose their licenses. The alternative is they could tragically wrap themselves around a tree and one of the parents could end up identifying his or her child on a cold slab in a morgue. Please don't let this happen to you or one of your friends, for life is precious and you have great potential and many years of possibilities for the future.

If you notice one of your friends behaving irresponsibly and driving erratic, speak up and tell them to wake up and stop being a jerk.

CHAPTER 15

HIGHER POWERS

So Who Is God?

Today a lot of people can't fathom who God is. They argue because they can't see Him. Well, you can't see gravity, electricity, or the wind, but you know it's there.

What holds the Sun up the sky millions of light years away? What stops it from falling to earth and burning us all up? There has to be something more powerful and magnificent than any of us can imagine. Scientific theories say we were formed by a tiny speck, developed into a tadpole, formed legs, then walked from an ape, and progressed to form eventually a human man as we know today. Well, why didn't all the apes form into a man? I'd say those apes left behind feel cheated and are ticked off. Don't you marvel at the miracle of how a baby is formed from two human cells, male and female, joined together? It's amazing that the cells keep dividing and growing into tissues and then organs that form the nine body systems.

Just be astonished by the hormone oxytocin that's released and contracts the uterus during childbirth and stimulates the mammary glands to eject milk during lactation. By the time the baby takes its first breath, a life begins all on its own. Just for a few minutes, marvel at all the activity that your body is capable of doing, or the creation of the universe with the formation of its precious gems, minerals, oil, gases, mountains, oceans, etc. The majority of people say, "I'm here for a good time, not a long time, and then I'll die and go to hell and party with all my friends."

So why are we here, for what purpose?

I believe there must be something bigger than we could ever imagine. What your parents and others believe in will have an influence on your perception of the whole religious theme. God created us with a free will. We have the ability to make our own decisions and choose the life we want to live. Ultimately, God wants you and me to make the choice to love Him with all your heart, soul, and body. There are many religious people who still get married or have their children baptized in the church.

When asked if we are a Christian, we might say yes, for I worship God on Sundays at church, while for the rest of the week we don't even give God any-more thought. Or we might not go to a church building at all to worship God.

But who is to say what's right or wrong? You are the church, not the building. Your body is the temple where God resides. You can commune with God in nature or at home any hour of the day or night. It is not necessary to belong to a certain domination. But it is desirable to attend church. It's where you can grow and be of service and encouragement to others. Reading and studying your Bible, hearing the word of God, and praying every day is like clothing yourself with protective armour from the sins and temptations of the world.

Even if you don't know how to pray, just saying the Lord's Prayer or talking to God like you're speaking to a friend is effective. God is power, and there is no problem that God can't solve. He knows everything. God is listening, He can hear you, and He will give you the answer in his own time, not in your time, so you need to be patient.

I'll tell you a story. When my children were little, we had a swimming pool built in the backyard of our home. The neighbours' backyard backed onto our backyard, and in their yard grew a huge gum tree with overhanging branches.

When the strong, westerly winds blew, some of the smaller branches and leaves would fall into our backyard and pool. Cleaning up was tiresome, and after a year, I finally cracked and approached my neighbour if we could get some of the overhanging branches loped off. The idea was refused, and then I approached the local council and submitted an application to have the tree cut back. Council said I needed to arrange a mediation meeting between council, the neighbours, and myself. I thought about this further and made a decision not to go ahead with the mediation. I then prayed to God for His intervention to do something and then never thought anymore about it. We eventually placed the home on the market after about a year, and it was sold and we moved away from the area.

Later I learned that the big-gumtree had been stuck by lightning and all that remained was a stump. How's that for God answering my prayer! Coincidence or luck, you might say, but I believe God is in control always, and this reinforced my faith.

God is real. He watches over us and has our back. He takes care of every little detail and concern we have. You can choose to ignore God's love for you and think you are not worthy enough, but He accepts you just the way you are.

God is our heavenly Father who created the world. His son called Jesus lived on earth, and when Jesus died, He was resurrected and now is with God. So we were not left alone, God sent us the Holy Spirit. The Holy Spirit or Holy Ghost is another person who resides within those who accept Jesus is our saviour and the biblical story. The Holy Spirit is to guide, intercede, protect, and comfort us.

You could be from another faith, as there are all different denominations. All have different customs, ideas, and interpretations of what the truth is. Some don't eat particular foods or drink alcohol and strong substances, like tea or coffee. Dancing is forbidden, such as belly dancing or salsa. Some don't gamble or buy raffle tickets.

Religion can have so many rules and regulations, so it's no wonder people are turning away from Christianity. Even some religious sects won't talk to others because they are not of the same faith.

If we worship the one God, why so many contradictions? If ten people read the same Bible scriptures, you possibly would have ten different various interpretations. I don't know or have all the answers to a lot of things, but I do know that I am nothing without God in my life. When I became a born-again Christian, I was fourteen years old, and I was filled with the Holy Spirit.

I made a commitment to God, but I was a lukewarm Christian, sitting on the fence, still in the world and afraid of what others might say.

Through my teenage years, I made decisions that sometimes included God but hardly read my Bible or prayed daily. When God wasn't the centre of my life, the devil was lurking in the shadows, and I made really stupid decisions. If you don't know who the devil is, he is depicted in cartoons as the guy in the red leotard suit with the horns, a long tail, and pitchfork, and he is the bad guy, the fallen angel.

Satan is very real, hell is very real, and Satan and his fallen angels will be cast into the lake of fire (hell).

Sin is sin. Doesn't matter if you told a little white lie or you stole a top from the local clothing store. It doesn't matter if you weren't caught, - God sees and knows everything. When I am weak and fall into temptation and sin, then God isn't going to like it. And just as your earthly father or mother will chastise you, you're going to be corrected by God, your Heavenly Father, also. It's not going to be something you can't handle, for God loves you and never gives us anything we can't handle.

To complicate things, Satan will twist your mind into believing your worthless and useless, and he will make you feel guilty and shameful person. This is exactly how the devil wants you to feel, and he will then leave you alone, because you're not going to be an effective Christian and will cower into the background. The devil is the prince of lies and deceit, and he is always ready to devour anyone in his path.

He has lots of names mentioned right throughout the Bible. I write these words not to frighten you, for God does not promise you an easy life where you will have no challengers as a Christian.

But He does promise you a way of handling any difficult situation, big or small, in your life. In Revelations, the last book in the Bible refers to the war between God and the devil. The war has already been won by God, so we have the power and the authority to defeat the devil whenever he tries to manipulate as into temptation in this life's battles or situations. We need to shout at the devil and tell him to go away and leave us alone.

My mistake was I forgot about God and thought I could handle my situations all by myself and fell into sin. You know when that little voice in your head says, "Don't do it," that was God talking to me, but I didn't want to listen, because I wanted to do things my own way.

If I had one thing to say to my younger self, I would say, "Listen to God and obey without questioning. Just do it. He loves you. He promises that He will never leave you. He wants the best for you, and He supplies all your needs. Be committed, loyal, and faithful to God's causes, with a burning desire to please and love God with all your heart, soul, and mind."

There are many different religions in the world, and your family and friends will be the biggest influence in your life. Ask questions about why people believe in their faith and why they have certain rituals. My aim is not to dishonour the different religious beliefs if they are different than mine, for that is not my intention. But I do have an obligation to tell you about God, His son Jesus Christ, who paid the price of our sins by dying on the cross, was resurrected and sits on the right side of God the Father in heaven. The everlasting treasures in heaven are waiting for everyone who believes and commits their life of obedience and faithfulness to God.

My religion is very simple. My religion is kindness.

-The Dalai Lama

Don't judge: rather forgive, accept or try to understand.

-Unknown

The Super Heroes

Everyone loves the superheroes. You probably have watched the movies, bought and swapped the comics, and played with action figures. The action heroes such as Superman, Spider Man, Wonder Woman, and the Hulk are all fictitious superheroes. You might say your dad is your real superhero. The real superheroes are the archangels and angels, the peace light workers of the world.

The Angels or Light Workers
Photo @ Malize/Dreamtime.com

These are the divine helpers, and you can call on them anytime to communicate with you. Angels are all around us. They are not to be prayed to or worshiped, because they are God's messengers.

Archangel Michael is an almighty angel who dispels fear and evil in the world. He gives you the courage and strength to achieve greater works.

Archangel Gabriel is the messenger angel who visited Mary and told her she was pregnant with God's child, if you are familiar with the biblical story. The prophet Mohammed was visited by Archangel Gabriel while he was living in a cave. Mohammed wrote the Islamic scripture, the Koran, receiving revelations from Gabriel. A powerful and strong archangel, and those that call on him will be pushed into action. Archangel Raphael role is to support, heal, and guide in matters of health. He can help you eliminate stress and negative thinking.

Call on Archangel Uriel for wisdom before you make any decisions and give you clarity to recognize dangerous situations. You can let go of destructive emotions such as anxiety and anger.

Archangel Jophiel is the angel of beautiful thoughts and will help you discover more about the beauty of God's holiness. There are many angels around us. Some are cute, little cherubs.

I had just visited a friend and was driving across a two-lane road to reach the median strip. There was a slight rise on the road, but I made sure there was no traffic on my right, and I proceeded to cross. All of a sudden, my instincts kicked in, and out of the corner of my eye I spotted a speeding car, so I jumped on my brakes and stopped short of the second lane. I had avoided the driver from smashing into my side of the car, and the driver continued on as if nothing happened. I proceeded to the median strip to stop, with my heart pounding so fast I thought it would leap straight out my chest. I believe God had sent me his angels to watch over me and minister to me, and I feel so blessed to have escaped this accident.

Maybe you know of someone who has had a similar experience,

for there are countless examples of God's and the angel's interventions or actions that aren't humanly possible and unexplainable.

Just recently my daughter's family lost their two dogs on a Friday afternoon after they escaped out of their backyard. I prayed to God that the puppies would be found as it was very upsetting for the family.

One of the dogs, a female called Storm, was rescued that night, and the next day the search was resumed to find Titan, the male dog. My daughter began to think that Titan must have been taken by somebody, because when she walked Storm, the dog began growling at every man as they passed along the way. Storm had never done this before, so it was distressful to think a stranger may have abducted little Titan and what if he was being mistreated. By early Sunday afternoon, it hadn't even occurred to me to ask for help from Archangel Gabriel, as well as being a messenger he or she also looks after children and animals.

Later on Sunday afternoon, maybe around 3:00 p.m., my daughter received a phone call from her girlfriend who had gone shopping that she had found Titan. Apparently the friend had confronted a man standing outside the local shopping centre with the dog. Amazingly, my daughter's friend was right there at the right place and the right time. You may say luck or coincidence, but I believe the angels had arranged this meeting between this man and my daughter's friend. Happy to say, Mum, Dad, my three granddaughters, and their two dogs are once more a family together.

As I have said, Satan or the devil is very real, although the church leaders preach very little about this fallen angel in their Sunday sermons.

Satan was the highest of the angels who rebelled against God because of his pride, and he desired to be God and not a servant. After the rebellion, Satan was cast out of heaven, convincing one third of the angels (now referred to as demons) to go with him. Demons exist in the invisible spirit realm yet affect the world physically. In our scientific, rational age, spiritual beliefs are scorned as just myths, and Satan doesn't care if you reject the whole fallen angel story as long as you're not following God. Satan is powerful and intelligent and entices many people to follow him, through their ignorance and confusion. He is the prince of lies and will deceive people, anytime you want to better yourself in any area of your life Satan will come up against you. But through God we can have the victory, because we have power now to resist Satan (www.allaboutgod.com/history-of-satan.htm).

CHAPTER 16

· · · · · · · · · · · · · · · · · ·

THE HIGHER POWER OF POLITICS

Once you reach eighteen years old as an Australian citizen, and you have lived at your current address for at least a month, you are required by law to vote. You can apply to have your name placed on the electoral role and then can vote in all the federal, state, and local elections.

You can enrol online through the Australian Electoral Commission or at your local member address. Once you have your name on the electoral roll and you fail to vote without a valid reason, such as being a patient in hospital, infirm, unable to leave workplace, then you will be fined. A lot of young people who are eighteen years old just can't be bothered voting or even to enrol as they think it is an unnecessary chore. And I did feel that way too until I realized it's a privilege to vote for candidates who have the best interest in governing the people for the future benefit for us all. If you look at the history of Australian politics, you will find that not all persons were allowed to vote and this right was only available for a few select people. But before this, in the early years, white settlement in Australia, British law was carried out by governors, who were given instructions by the Parliament in London. People in Australia had no say in making the laws, but they had to obey them. Then gradually Australians set up their first Parliament, and they did have a say in the laws. They won the right to vote, although only men who owned a substantial lot of property could.

From 1850, the Australian colonies were given the right to govern themselves. They made laws about who could vote or not, and you needed to be over twenty-one years old. Indigenous men were not encouraged to enrol and vote but were not denied the right to vote.

By the Federation, January 1, 1901, the colonies by arrangement were joined together to form a single nation, the Australian Commonwealth, and the colonies would become states.

Edmond Barton became Australia's first prime minister. As established by the Constitution of Australia, the Parliament of Australia is composed of two houses, the House of Representatives and the Senate, together with the Queen. The monarch is represented through the governor general, who has executive powers granted in the Constitution. The governor general is removable by the Queen on the advice of the prime minister.

In 1902, the Commonwealth Franchise Act passed, enabling all women (with the exception of aboriginal women in some states) to vote for the federal parliament.

Interestingly women from the different states were allowed to vote but were introduced during different periods, which I found typical of male domination. Notice the range of time periods to vote of the following: 1895, South Australia; 1899, Western Australia; 1902, New South Wales; 1905, Queensland; 1908, Victoria; 1911 Northern Territory and Canberra.

Parliament met for the first time in Melbourne on May 9, 1901, with seventy-five members of the House of Representatives and thirty-six senators (six for each state). In 1962, the Commonwealth Electoral Act was amended so that indigenous people could enrol to vote in federal elections if they wanted to. For all other Australians it was compulsory to enrol. It was also an offence for anyone to place pressure or influence Aborigines to enrol, because once enrolled, it was compulsory for them to vote.

Women in Federal and State Parliament

This is not an extensive list of all women who have contributed effectively in the roles of the political arena, and my apologies if your name is missing.

- 1884 Victoria's Henrietta Dugdale formed the first Australian Women's Suffrage Society in Melbourne
- 1897 South Australian Catherine Spence, first woman to stand as political candidate in Australia. She stood as SA delegate to the federal convention, however even if she had won, she could not have sat.
- 1921- Western Australia's Edith Cowan elected to Legislative Assembly as member for West Perth, the first woman elected to any Australian Parliament
- 2007 - Anna Bligh elected the first female premier of Queensland
- 2008 – First female governor- general of Australia Quentin Bryce who later became Dame Quentin Bryce
- 2010 - First female Julia Gillard became prime minister
- 2013 - First indigenous woman Nova Peris to be elected to the federal government, representing the Northern Territory. Nova represented Australia and is a Olympic hockey gold medal winner
- 2016 - Linda Burney, winning the seat of Barton to become the first Aboriginal woman elected to the federal lower house

Voting

Voting is held at least every three years and always on a Saturday between the hours of 8:00 a.m. and 6:00 p.m. If you are travelling/ overseas, you can elect to vote early by postal vote, which you can pick up from the Australian Post outlet, or the Australian Electoral Commission can mail you a voting pack. If you do vote this way, then you will need to have a witness who will oversee your vote and sign the paper.

If you are in need of assistance because you are legally blind, deaf, or have a hearing or speech impairment, then the National Relay Service Interpreter Service is available.

You elect a particular political party to govern this country for a term of office of three years. There are many political parties, the Australian Liberal Party, Australian Labour Party, Australian Democratic, and the Greens. And there are many minor parties, such as the Shooters Party, the Christian Party, and the 4WD Party, just to name some. A politician needs to win his electoral seat and retain office and this means his or her focus is to rely on marginal seats and swinging voters as well. It is within these parties, whether Labour, Liberal, or the Greens, that the politicians vote in the preferred leader of their party.

Whoever is appointed as their leader, they may not serve out their three years of office, as within the party there maybe unrest and criticism, and even prime ministers have been stripped of rank and been dismissed. And, in the case of Prime Minister Gogh Whitlam in 1975, the Australian governor general, Sir John Kerr, dismissed him and appointed Malcolm Fraser of the Liberal Party as caretaker prime minister.

And who can forget the fiasco of the first female prime minister of Australia, Julia Gillard, being dismissed within her own Labour Party? It seemed like a three-ring circus if you watched the televised sessions and the behaviour in Parliament House. It was reality TV with all the drama, and it was within their own party who first voted them into office.

For those politicians who have the Australian public in their best interests, they have done a sterling job and deserve accolades.

For a federal election, you are voting to elect people to represent you in the two houses of the Australian parliament, the House of Representatives and the Senate.

You will receive two ballot papers:

- Green representative in your local area in the local area in the House of Representatives
- White representative of your state or territory in the Senate

On the ballot paper, the form has an optional preferential vote, you can either vote above the black line, numbering your first choice preferred political party, or below the line, numbering your preferred candidates.

On election night, counting of votes is known as a scrutiny, and those observing are called scrutineers, and they, are nominated by the candidates. Scrutineers have a right to be present when the ballot boxes are sealed or opened and when the votes are sorted and counted.

A candidate can appoint one scrutineer for each polling place so they may check for possible irregularities. They may enter and leave the polling places at any time, during the counts of which they can be replaced, and they can inspect any ballot paper. Scrutineers may not enter polling place without a completed appointment form or an identification badge. They cannot help remove any material from polling booths or interfere with or attempt to influence any elector. But they may be nominated by an elector to help with the completion of a ballot paper. There is a handbook with a more comprehensive list of dos and don'ts that a scrutineer should be familiar with before he or she participates in the roll.

I have only given you some points of the important duties they have on Election Day. On Election Day, you may be required to vote for the House of Representatives, a referendum, and the Senate. A referendum is a question that asks the Australian voters if they would like an amendment on a controversial subject. For example, "Do the Australian people want to become a republic and no longer be under the British monarchy?" or "Do the Australian people agree that it is acceptable to have same sex marriages?"

The vote counting is always done in this order:

1. House of Representatives
2. Referendum (if required)
3. Senate

After 6.00 p.m. sharp, the polling places close and the polling officials are required to complete the following:

- Count the first preference votes on House of Representatives
- Conduct a two candidate preferred on the House of Representatives
- Count the first preference vote on Senate papers
- Count and sort any declaration vote envelopes received on the day

Again, I do not want to overload you with too much information. There is a lot that goes into planning an election, and the responsibilities are enormous for the candidates and the many people behind the scenes who have different jobs to do.

So the right thing that you and I can do is to be a voice, place our formal votes in the ballot boxes, and hopefully make the best contribution with politicians running this country.

For the first time, voters in the 2016 federal election will see a small logo next to the party name on the Senate ballot paper.

Interestingly those candidates you vote for will receive money in the pocket for every person who votes for them. No wonder the politicians are out in force speaking with the public before elections, promising everyone the star on the Christmas tree(en.Wikipedia.org/wiki/1975_australian_constitutional_crisis)http://www.smh.com.au/federal-election-2016/will-the-best-logo-win-analysing-senate-ballot-paper).

The Australian Bureau of Statistics conducts a census data of all those living in Australia every four years. This data helps shape the future of Australia, with infrastructure in building roads and schools for the needs of the people and gathers other information.

On August 9, 2016, the systems computer site was hacked, and as a precautionary step to protect Australians' data, the online system was taken down. The newly elected government headed by Prime Minister Malcolm Turnbull was embarrassed and angry with the debacle.

CHAPTER 17

TACKLING MENTAL HEALTH

B eing well-balanced in life, emotionally, physically, mentally, and spiritually, is the ideal dream for us to be joyful. Don't be overloaded with multitasking. Do one thing at a time, finish the task, and then move on. Stress is caused by what's going on inside and all around us, and how we react to circumstances. For instance, we may have heard something negative about ourselves. We can react by getting angry, going into a rage, and self-harming.

Adolescent Girl Upset
Photo @Aleksey Gorbatenkov/Dreamtime.com

Another way is to hold the belief we must not allow ourselves to feel emotions we deem negative, such as fear, rage, depression, guilt, and shame. But what we resist and repress tends to surface anyway, and our bodies become sick. Every noticed, if you are embarrassed, you might blush, sweat, and become tongue-tied? We cannot lie to ourselves, so don't sweep emotions under the carpet and hope no one notices. Hurdles are a normal part of life and help is always available. Allow yourself to open up to your parents or carers and start talking. You will find that, deep down, they truly love you and want the best for you, even though their actions might not express this.

There is a saying: "You have to be cruel to be kind." And what this means, is sometimes adults force you to face up to your own responsibilities. Pushing you into helping yourself, even though you don't like it, it will allow you to grow up faster. Some parents are helicopter parents and always hovering around and doing everything for their teenagers when they are capable of doing things for themselves. Be grateful you don't have helicopter parents, as it shows they don't trust your judgement and capabilities.

Journaling is a fantastic therapy release for unleashing your emotions, just write down how you feel every day. It will help set you free. Trying to be everybody's best friend and overcommitting yourself will lead to feeling overwhelmed, so you need to learn to say no to others. If you're feeling like you want to hurt yourself or others, these are serious issues, and you should seek help immediately. If you are or suspect someone is cutting their body, the tell-tale signs are changes in mood or their sleep and eating patterns.

Covering up with long sleeves on a very hot day is one tell-tale sign of a cutter, although the person maybe covering because he or she doesn't want to get sunburnt. Less common mental health illnesses are schizophrenia and bipolar mood disorder. People live in a fantasy world, lose touch with reality, and can't make sense of their thoughts and feelings.

A psychotic episode can involve delusions, false beliefs of persecution, guilt or grandeur. The person may see things, hear voices, or taste things that are not there, and this can be confusing and threatening to others. There is a stigma associated with mental illness, and feelings of shame, blame, hopelessness, and distress occur. It causes people to hide their symptoms, mood swings, and depression as they are treated differently, they are excluded and feel isolated from others.

Schizophrenia is a serious brain disorder marked by changes in cognitive and emotional function. Its causes are marked by genetics, environment, and brain chemistry, history of abuse, or neglect.

Cognitive symptom is the inability to process information, focusing, memory, learning anything new, and making decisions.

Bipolar disorder is a mental illness with more extreme mood swings that lasts-longer, and the person finds it hard to function in everyday life. There are two types, mania and depression. The mania is high energy, talkative, overconfident, behaves recklessly, grandiose beliefs, and lasts at least a week.

The depressive type lasts at least two weeks. The person finds it hard to concentrate, loses interest, withdraws from people, has feelings of worthiness, has difficulty in sleeping, and is suicidal.

Bipolar disorder affects a person's judgement, with unrealistic perceptions and beliefs about their own abilities.

Morgellons disease is a delusional disorder that leads to the belief that the person has parasites or foreign matter moving in or coming out of his or her skin. I worked with someone who would scratch her skin till she bled and sores formed. Before her diagnoses, she said it felt like insects crawling under her skin, and unfortunately, there is no specific cure.

Anxiety disorders include post-traumatic stress, social phobias, agoraphobia, panic disorder and obsessive-compulsive disorder. It's normal to be anxious performing on stage, making speeches, during exam times and job interviews, and nothing for you to be concerned with health-wise. It's when it becomes habitual and you can't cope with simple tasks that you should pay attention. If your health professional has prescribed medication, they will require you to obtain regular blood tests to monitor that your drug levels are correct. You may have good intentions of taking yourself off your medications because you feel better, but this is never a good idea.

When patients don't take their meds this can lead to destructive behaviour to yourself and others causing serious harm and even death. Perhaps you will be on your drugs for the rest of your life allowing you to function normally.

Suicide

Suicidal rates are increasing every year, the statistics are alarming, and Australian indigenous adolescents are five times more likely to commit suicide. Late July 2016, two males, one nineteen years old, Stuart Kelly, and the other fifteen years old, in year ten, Louis Doulougeris, committed suicide. So tragic for everyone who knew these young men, and what is sad is that Stuart Kelly was the brother of Thomas Kelly, the victim of the cowardly king-hit punch attack that I mentioned in chapter 3. Statically, there is at least one suicide every week. This is extremely alarming and a national disgrace. It can be tough if you live in remote areas or you are a refugee and language is a barrier or if you don't make friends easily.

The Internet can be a tempting place to spend all your time, but it's important to build relationships with face-to-face friendships. Youth in foster care and juvenile settings are at a 40 percent greater risk of becoming homeless within twelve months than other people according to the "Transitioning from Care Report."

The federal government and corporations have funded millions of dollars in grants to address the problem. We are failing the majority of today's youth and the government, society, schools, parents, doctors, medical professionals, and churches are all to blame.

Possible Warning Signs

- Thinking, talking, and writing about death

- Withdrawing from all social interactions
- Increase in substance abuse
- Regularly self-harming
- Giving your possessions away to others
- Doing dangerous stunts
- Moods change erratically

This is a list of helpful organizations' websites and phone numbers if you or you know someone who needs help in crisis: **If it's an emergency, then phone 000** or on your **mobile 112**

1. Head Space - 1800 650 890, www.headspace.org.au
2. Beyond Blue – 1300224636, www.beyondblue.org.au
3. Kids Helpline - 1800 55 1800, www.kidshelpline.com.au
4. ReachOut.com - online website
5. Sane Australia - 1800 18 7263
6. Suicide Call Back Service - 1300 659 467, www.suicidecallback service.org.au
7. Lifeline - 13 11 14, www.lifeline.org.au

Talk to a teacher, counsellor, or trusted friend if you are feeling down in the dumps, anxious, depressed, if you're having thoughts of suicide, or if you just need someone to listen to you. Obviously too many young people in the community are falling between the cracks.

You can't make a quick fix, such as doctors prescribing antidepressants, and not follow-up with counselling sessions. The Medicare health system will allow ten free counselling sessions.

The problems facing the youth of today are unemployment with no real direction, no incentives for getting a job, not enough apprenticeships offered, and outrageous fees for higher education for an ordinary person. Pushing the retirement age up to seventy years of age is hard for workers who are already doing hard manual work. Bring back the retiring age to sixty, let those who are fitter, younger and healthier to be placed in employment. Work gives people self-esteem and confidence, something to be proud of and a sense that they are productive and contributing to society in a positive direction.

Do you ever feel that something isn't right, you're not good enough, you feel alone, life is just too hard, no one understands you, you feel like a failure, everything you do is wrong, you're a freak, your boring, you're not pretty enough, or you just feel down? It is not uncommon for any of us to have these feelings.

Over thinking

- I'm too skinny.
- I wonder if I'm gay.
- I have a drug problem.
- I'm getting bullied.
- I have an alcohol problem.
- I hate myself.
- I feel angry all the time.
- I feel unhappy.
- I'm being sexually abused.
- No one likes me.

Maybe you are depressed, and you are overwhelmed by others or your circumstances. Most of the time we are comparing ourselves to others. We see that others are having a great time, and they're happy and full of life. But in reality it may be just a big, fat lie, and they are putting up a good front. Nobody can be 100 percent happy and without problems all the time, you and I will always have issues, but it's our attitudes and how we handle them that matter.

How can you help yourself if you feel depressed?

1. Have a good healthy diet - no junk food.

2. Make sure you're doing some exercises such as walking or swimming out in the fresh air.
3. Try to get a good night's sleep.
4. Start journaling every day – just write down your thoughts and feeling; it's important to be honest with yourself.
5. Make sure your connecting with family and friends in a positive way.
6. Abstain from drugs or alcohol, this makes the situation worse.
7. Practice relaxing and meditation, learn yoga.
8. Clean up your surroundings, get the clutter out.
9. Practice some deep breathing.
10. Stop comparing yourself to others.
11. Drink plenty of water.
12. Get outside and walk on the ground or sand with bare feet.
13. Repeat these words out aloud: "I am enough."
14. Remember all the blessings in your life and be thankful and grateful.
15. Laughter is the outward evidence of inward joy. It lifts our spirits and dispels worry, anxiety, and depression. Make a daily routine of laughing improves emotional and mental health.

The media has a dreadful habit of putting a negative spin on world events, and that negativity can be highly contagious. Keep up with current affairs, but don't be consumed by watching and listening to the news.

I started writing in my health journal after I fractured three bones in my ankle in late 2015 from a fall while on holidays. I struggled with keeping weight off my injured foot for six weeks and laid in bed with my foot elevated on pillows. I was useless on my crutches and hobbled around on one foot till I could bear weight on the injured foot.

My confidence was shattered, and my bed was my sanctuary, as I never ventured anywhere except to doctors' appointments for four months. I was angry with myself - if only I had taken a plane flight to my destination, instead of travelling by car; If only I walked in the rain wearing my joggers instead of sandals; if only.

Well, I can't rewind those decisions I made, and neither can you change past events. We can only learn from our choices and accept situations by coming to terms with our feelings and moving into positive states of mind.

During the rehabilitation period, the little meltdowns and tears flowed, but I knew I just had to try and keep moving through the emotional pain and physical pain of doing exercises. Within those months of anger and frustrations, I finally learnt to lean on God by letting go and accepting the situation. Simply writing down on paper my feelings and thoughts every day, whether they were good or bad, was a healing process.

I still continue to write in my journal every week and write down the things that I'm grateful for.

Remember: if you need immediate help, phone a friend or, in an emergency, call 000.

CHAPTER 18

EDUCATION AND JOB INTERVIEWS

Nothing is more important than your own self-belief and valuing yourself. Gaining higher education and learning new things, with the ultimate aim of self-satisfaction, leads to success, fulfilment and happiness. Regardless of your age, ethnic origins, prior education, religion, or disability, it's possible for all Australian adolescents to have the best education. Self-confidence is not something you are born with; it's something you develop as you go through life.

When you were a baby, nobody told you that you can't walk. In fact - your parents and everybody else encouraged you to try. You fell down, hurting yourself many times, but you just kept pulling yourself back up until you could eventually walk.

School

It's the same with school. Teachers will be encouraging you to learn, and one day it all gets easier and you start getting good results. Learn, revise, study, practice, and with determination, you can get that D grade to a B+, the one you deserved because of all your hard work.

Now if you absolutely hate school and start being disruptive in class, your classmates will laugh at your foolish antics. Your class teacher won't be impressed, and neither will the principal. Unfortunately for your classmates, when it comes to exam time, panic and fear will be etched on their faces. That's the reason for school, to learn. It's a privilege denied to many in the world even today, especially for girls. You only have to read the story about Malala, the human rights activist from Pakistan who was shot by the Taliban for speaking about the right to an education for girls.

Some countries don't have the resources to even educate boys, and so girls have no chance. You are one of the lucky ones, as education is relatively free, and you have the choice to further your education by attending university or tafe college or gaining an apprenticeship or traineeship.

And one thing I have learnt is that you can never stop learning. New innovative ideas and techniques are forever changing, whether you've been doing the same job for twenty-five years. This is a story of a close friend who disliked school and wasn't academically gifted but had lots of common sense and personality. His mum said, "If you can find a job, then you can leave school," and so he found work as a tyre fitter in a service station at the age of fifteen. He soon realized that, to make it in this world and to earn more money, he needed to better himself.

He seized the opportunity to change his job to a bigger company, and he progressed to become a crane chaser. Then, furthering his ambitions, he changed to a different company and career, where he became skilled in driving trucks, dozers, excavators, and other mechanical equipment.

So if you think that you don't have any chance of improving your job prospects or you have no opportunity for advancement, think again. With the right attitude and determination, the doors will start opening for you. The universe provides you with the right people just to come along at the right time to help make your dreams reality. Break the limiting belief that you're not good enough. Don't dumb yourself down. Confront your anxieties and difficulties head on. Find books or videos. Talk to others who have the knowledge you need to further your career.

Comparing yourself to others in a positive way does have its advantages, because it will help you improve yourself. The negative way is to say, "I can't do that. I can't be bothered. No use trying, it won't work."

Ever noticed in your class the top two students are always trying to beat the other one. That's good competition. One always seems to have the edge over the other one, then bang, the one that's always coming in second gets the top mark at the yearly exam.

University

University is another world, you are pretty much left to your own learning here, for the academics believe you have the maturity to learn on your own terms. Yes, there is help, but you're not treated like a baby; no one is going to hold your hand. If you want to cut classes and goof off, well, you are not going to pass your exams and get your degree. University education isn't free in Australia, and unless you get a scholarship, it can be quite expensive. The government allows you to pay back a student loan after you're earning over the threshold of a certain amount of money.

But remember: every exam you fail you will need to re-sit. It's going to cost you more money and will be added onto your already high fees. A few years ago, I met an inspirational young lady (my hairdresser at the time) who obtained an apprenticeship as a hairdresser at the age of sixteen. She became a fully qualified hairdresser, and then she started university as a mature-age student to obtain her degree in primary education as a schoolteacher. So she not only had a trade which provided a part-time income while studying for her degree, but also she was only twenty-three years old.

Working Life

Another example is me, a young, ambitious seventeen-year-old and a trainee student nurse who lived in the nurses' accommodation at the local hospital. Nurses today are educated through the university system. They also work in the hospitals gaining practical experience. When I was nursing in the hospital system, nurses were rostered on shifts in the different wards working morning or late shifts. Every three or four months, we had four weeks of block education training and were tutored by education nursing sisters. Night shifts were worked in complete four-week blocks, and with theatre work, you participated on night and weekend call-outs.

Two other nurses and I were on call for theatre one night, and there were two emergencies. We worked tirelessly from 11: 00 p.m. to 3:00 a.m. and after finishing as we were walking back to the nursing home, we actually got bailed up by the night watchman as he was doing his rounds. Thinking we were just getting home from a night out, he wanted to know where we had been. I thought, you must be kidding; we are in our nurses' uniforms. Anyway, we sorted it out, and arriving back very tired at the nurses' quarters, we managed to get some shut-eye, only to be awakened by the alarm clock at 5:45 a.m. to get ready to start the day shift at 6.30 a.m.

It was a good life, but you were tired from shift work and the quick shifts. I lived away from home, three meals per day, my nurse's uniforms laundered and starched, and my room was cleaned. I was totally independent. I had freedom when I wasn't working and could easily walk to the beach, cafes, and shopping centres. My traineeship was a total of three years, and if I qualified and became a registered nurse, I could further my studies and become a midwife.

But what did I do? Resigned after twenty months and lost sight of my dream of a nursing career. My focus was on fun times now. I didn't read and research enough of my textbooks. When I needed to study for an exam, I panicked. There wasn't enough time to cram any study in as well as working, and I totally screwed up. I actually don't even know if I even passed my last exams. All I had to do was talk to someone, open up about my feelings, but I made a wrong choice and didn't show up for my next shift.

All I had to do was stay focused, knuckle down, and complete the course, just another sixteen months to go. Looking back now, I think I was heading for a nervous breakdown, trying to burn the candle at both ends. Set your intention on finishing the course or project, and you will be the winner. There is help available in all schools, university, and workplaces, if you need to talk to somebody.

If you don't like the work you're doing, tick it off and find something else you want to try. Don't get stuck for the next forty years in a job you hate because you'll have a mediocre life. Love the work you do, and it won't seem like work at all.

Of course, not all work involves study, so no matter what kind of work you do, apply yourself and be the best checkout chick, cook, chef, cleaner, shop person, police officer, horse jockey, nanny, or aged-care nurse. It all comes down to your attitude and determination. Believe in yourself. You are capable of reaching your dreams. Keep focusing on your goals that's on your vision board.

Be Your Own Entrepreneur

If you have a dream of being your own boss, then congratulations for making a gutsy choice, it will be hard work, with many hours in the early part but it can be very profitably to own a business. Passion is something that can motivate you into action. Procrastination is something that prevents you from living your passion and deprives you of achieving your dreams. Procrastination is where you intend to do something but somehow never get around to doing it by making excuses.

By procrastinating you are reaffirming the belief that you can't achieve your goals. Identify those self-limiting beliefs that are holding you back. No successful person ever got to where he or she is by doing nothing. There is nothing stopping you from achieving your dreams and goals. Being your own boss is a big commitment, hard work, long hours to start with, dedication, persistence, and patience. You may work alone or have employees who work for you, so you will have a few different roles to play. You will never stop learning and growing as a person, achieving success financially hopefully, but you will certainly gain personal development.

Job Interviews

Everyone will probably do one or two job interviews at least in their working life unless you will be placed in the family business or unable to work because of medical reasons. Interviews are daunting and confronting, usually with a panel of the company's personnel, one being the boss and HR manager and another two persons, possibly department managers. You only have at least twenty minutes to make a great impression, and the first few minutes with be crucial. For much of your twelve years of schooling, and maybe beyond, you will have been working towards this very moment of being interviewed for a job.

Whatever the position you want there is a few rules to follow that will be helpful:

- Dress appropriately for a job interview. Nobody wants to see your disco outfit, boobs, or G-string underneath your see-through skirt. Dressing smart-casual in colours, blue, black, and taupe, white or grey, with coloured accessories is a good option. Hair should be clean and tidy and minimize jewellery pieces.
- Do not slouch in your chair. Good posture is needed. It shows confidence and do not chew bubble gum.
- Speak clearly. Don't mumble with your hand over your mouth and try not to say a lot of slang words and "ums."

Answer the questions to the best of your ability while looking directly at the person speaking to you.

These tips are highly sought after by an employer

- How well you can communicate with others and whether you interact effectively and form friendships with work colleagues after hours.
- How passionate you are about the position - it's no use applying for a job in a manufacturing company if you want to join the armed forces. Passion creates energy, persuades momentum, and it's recognized.
- The technical skills that you have obtained with hands-on experience, learning to type 180 words per minute, for example.
- The academic results - that's why exam results are important. The employer will know your qualifications are in line with the job description.
- Do you have any work experience? In year ten, you will have the opportunity to have work experience in your chosen field. This is why you do your absolute best. Results will depend on your attitude, character, and work. This is how you can shine and show a potential employer you're the right person for the job.
- Cultural fit - do you have the consideration for the differences in ethnic, sex, religious, disabilities, and show compassion to others who are different?
- Emotional intelligence - your boss wants to know if you can handle situations that call for maturity. If your employer has given you some work that is beyond your capabilities, what would he think if you had a hissy fit and cried? It takes maturity to just say, "I'm sorry, but I don't know how to do this. Can someone else do it or someone show me how please?"

- Teamwork is vitally important to any company and getting along with others shows an employer how you interact with others.
- Extracurricular activities that you are engaged in shows your employer that you have balance in your life. All work and no play makes for a very dull life, so engage in outside activities.
- An employer is looking for leadership qualities, those who are able to work alone and whether you show initiative when it comes to solving challenges or problems.

An employer is looking to see who is best for the position and not necessarily who is best academically. All of the above list is taken into the equation when sorting persons to fill jobs. Companies want the right fit, so what if you're not the sharpest tool in the tool shed, but you have a great personality and can play a competitive game of tennis doubles may just land that dream job. Yes, interviews are uncomfortable, and if you are really panicking, try deep breathing for a couple of minutes. This will calm your nerves before you go in for your interview. The interviewers who are on the panel are only human and understand that it is stressful to be in front of everyone.

Perhaps the night before, try visualizing the scenario. Play acting is a really good way of seeing how you can perform. Picture yourself on the centre of the stage and the interviewers are your audience. Act like you're in the performance of your life. Your Academy Award will be obtaining the job, so go out and party afterwards. And even if you didn't get the job, reward yourself anyway. The next time you go for an interview it will be easier.

Without a doubt interviews and exams are stressful but a necessary part of life, so just be yourself and relax. If you've done your homework and tried your best, that's all anybody can expect from you. Keep applying yourself. You have greatness within you, and that amazing day will arrive when all your hard work has paid off.

Think Positive
Photo @Flynt/Dreamtime.com

During your years at school, apply yourself to be the best you can be. We all can't be Albert Einstein (the genius), but if we try real hard, that's all any parent and teacher expects. Exam results don't reflect the total picture of someone's success, but they give you a good start in life. And that's my wish for you all, to be successful and happy in your school, careers, or jobs.

FINAL NOTE

My intention for this book is for you to gain the confidence to experience all of life that's on offer and to question everything. Don't make rash choices or impulse decisions. Give yourself enough time to think it all through clearly. It isn't about whatever decision you make, if it's right or wrong - it's about what feels true to you.

If you feel all knotted up inside and highly panicky about your decision, then this is confirmation that it's not right, authentic, or your true nature. It's normal to feel a little stress such as before making a speech or swimming free-style in the final race championships.

And if you find life or your decision hasn't worked out the way you wanted it to, just change the course in a different direction. Remember nothing needs to be set in concrete, face your fears, self-doubts, and overcome limiting beliefs that are keeping you stuck. You are good enough, so go after whatever you want in life and apply actions to reach the top of your mountain.

Blessings and gratitude,
Ann

Printed in the United States
By Bookmasters